The Country Diary Book of

FLOWERS

DRYING, PRESSING AND POT POURRI

THE COUNTRY DIARY BOOK OF

POSITION COUNTRY DIARY....

FLOWERS

DRYING, PRESSING AND POT POURRI

CAROL PETELIN

With photographs by
Simon McBride

Henry Holt and Company
New York

The publishers would like to thank Rowena Stott.
Edith Holden's great-niece and the owner of the original works,
who has made the publication of this book possible.

Originally published in Great Britain by
Webb & Bower (Publishers) Limited
9 Colleton Crescent, Exeter, Devon EX2 4BY

Library of Congress Catalog Card Number: 91–55133
ISBN 0–8050–1770–4

Henry Holt books are available at special discounts for bulk
purchases for sales promotions, premiums, fund-raising, or
educational use. Special editions or book excerpts can also be
created to specification.

For details contact:
Special Sales Director
Henry Holt and Company, Inc.
115 West 18th Street
New York, New York 10011

First American Edition

Designed by Sue Stainton

Printed and bound in Hong Kong Produced by Mandarin Offset

1 3 5 7 9 10 8 6 4 2

PAGE 1: an archway in a walled garden, looking
through to banks of fragrant lavender.

FRONTISPIECE: a basket of air-dried peonies waiting
to be arranged.

CONTENTS

INTRODUCTION

Flowers present us with one of nature's greatest fragrant and visual pleasures. They fill us with a wonderful sense of well-being, they remind us of special moments in our lives, and they make the loveliest of gifts for any occasion.

Each season holds it own charm, a charm that captivated Edith Holden earlier this century. She portrayed nature and her special discoveries in the countryside at their most appealing in her delightful texts and delicate paintings. Such refreshing simplicity has enamoured thousands of people to her beautiful books *The Country Diary of an Edwardian Lady* and the recently discovered *The Nature Notes of an Edwardian Lady*. Her writing and illustrations are a constant reminder of the abudance of floral material that is available for us to use and enjoy.

The precious items we may find during walks in the country can inspire us to make beautiful decorations for our families and friends. But always remember that many species of wild flowers are protected and may not be picked, so please check with the list on page 154 so that you do not break the law.

Spring is the season of renewal, and I think that it is the most magical time of the year as little plants push their way up through the damp earth. A shower of rain followed by the warming sun makes everything smell wonderfully heady and fresh. Banks of primroses and bluebells growing in lush green woods are such a contrast to the bland colours of the winter undergrowth. I can vividly remember the walks we went on when I was little, when we picked these wonderful flowers to take back home, filling every available vase and jam jar and carefully pressing some between the pages of a book, to be found, forgotten, months later.

Gardens too begin to show signs of life, with bulbs revealing pointed tips and leaves, tightly curled and rather pale in colour, clinging on to stems. Then great preparations begin as the garden is made ready for the planting of flowers for the summer. A garden is one of the most cherished of possessions. Anyone who is lucky enough to own even the smallest plot can produce some sort of offering that can be used in floral decorations or that can be preserved for later use or perhaps included in pot pourri.

Unlike cultivated flowers, which are relatively easy to dry, wild flowers do not enjoy being picked and stood in water, and they die quite quickly. They are harder than cultivated flowers to air dry, and only a few varieties will keep their colour. Some types, such as wild irises and orchids and some of the fleshier flowers, will dry most successfully in a desiccant such as silica gel, but the best way to preserve the more delicate varieties is to press them.

Children usually love to be given a small area of garden in which to plant their own seeds. This can present a wonderful challenge to them, and the gift of a flower press will encurge them to join in later on, when the time comes to make up ideas with flowers. This participation not only produces delightful results but can also enable you to teach them to learn the names of various plants and to love and respect nature from an early age.

Pressing flowers is rewarding. Flatter headed types press most successfully, while bulbous flowers tend to turn mouldy as the water is retained for too long. In the chapter on pressed flowers you will find a list of suitable plant material.

Once summer is here, we wish it could last forever. If the weather is good, we can spend much spare time outdoors, taking advantage of the long, light mornings and evenings. Summer is the time to enjoy our gardens and the countryside to the full, picking and harvesting as many types as possible. The flowers must be chosen care-

fully, for any blemishes will be accentuated after drying. During the summer make sure there is no blight on your plants, such as aphids, which cling to the stems and around the flower heads, ruining the petals, which wither and eventually die completely. A mild spray, preferably one of the organic formulations that have replaced the harsher insecticides, should be used to eliminate this problem. If you are lucky enough to have ladybirds in your garden, do not kill them as these pretty and useful insects will help to combat the pests. Slugs and caterpillars can also do untold damage to plants, and they particularly enjoy young plantlets!

Of all our senses, smell is probably the one that brings back the greatest memories. Wherever we are, we all love to be surrounded by pleasant scents; they give us a feeling of well-being and bring us great comfort. There are few things to surpass sitting on a warm summer's evening in the quiet of one's own garden, surrounded by the wonderfully intoxicating scent of flowers.

Summer is the time to pick and dry the greater bulk of flowers for use in later months. Most flowers are with us only briefly, so by preserving them, you can enjoy just as much visual pleasure as when they are fresh. Try experimenting with any types that please you; there really are very few flowers that cannot be preserved in some way.

Autumn is the season for gathering in. It is the time when you will be collecting last-minute materials from your garden or from the countryside, and it is also the time for clearing your garden and planting shrubs for the next year. By the time autumn is with us, many wild flowers will have lost their greenness, and you will be able to find numerous interesting skeletonized shapes to pick; dried hemlock, for example, which sometimes grows to incredible heights, can look stunning in a large pot on the floor. Spiky stems holding a variety of seed pods will add texture to more softly shaped garden flowers. Seed heads should be placed in a paper bag before being hung to dry to prevent a cascade of seeds falling on to the floor. Acorns and beech nuts will be quickly snatched by squirrels, so make sure you go early in autumn to hunt for them, as they are the perfect addition to an autumn display. They should be collected before they turn completely brown, when the nuts become loose in their shells.

During the winter months, when you find yourselves indoors, many a cold, wet afternoon can be spent making use of the specimens you have preserved earlier in the year. Carefully dried petals and herbs can be turned into bowls of sweet-smelling pot pourri, which will be wonderful gifts for either Christmas or some other special occasion. You could try your hand at creating a picture out of pressed flowers to cheer up a wall in your home. These and other ideas can be found by turning the pages of this book.

Winter is the time for reflection and planning. Each year brings greater experience in growing and drying and opportunities to correct past errors, and as you dig over your garden, work out a plan for the new year's planting.

This book is a guide to preserving all types of plant material, and it is designed to show you many ways of creating wonderful displays and flower crafts. There are ideas for each season, although naturally you can adapt the materials you have to form your own style, substituting one type of flower for another. Contact with flowers is such a gentle distraction, bringing us pleasant relief from this world full of tension and pressures, and I hope that the ideas contained in the pages that follow will encourage you to try to preserve some of the flowers from your own garden and to include them in arrangements for your own home and those of your friends.

PAGES 8-9: achilleas are available in a range of colours; these are being grown for drying.

GROWING
AND
HARVESTING

GROWING FLOWERS FOR DRYING

There are few things that can compare with an English country garden in full bloom. Borders that overflow with plants of every shape and colour, with hardly a patch of visible bare earth, are a never-failing source of pleasure. Gardens like these can be found with wonderful selections of old-fashioned flowers – hollyhocks, towering above delphiniums and their smaller cousin the larkspur, achilleas, love-in-a-mist, cornflowers, lavenders and roses to name but a few. The effect is stunning, and the fragrance of this mass of flowers is an overwhelming delight.

If you are fortunate enough to possess a garden, you could try turning part of it into a special area to grow flowers for drying so that you do not ruin the effect in the other beds and borders by over-picking. This area could be set out rather as you would lay out a vegetable garden, with the flowers planted in rows. A sheltered spot, ideally backed by a wall or fence, is best so that plants are not damaged by the wind. If you do not have additional space, you could try planting some extra flowers among your other plants to meet your additional requirements. These can usually be squeezed in somewhere, or, if space in the beds and borders is very restricted, you could grow plants in tubs or growing bags. Most flowers need sunshine, but some varieties prefer shade, so tubs or bags have the additional advantage that they can be placed accordingly.

You will require soil that is only mildly acidic to averagely alkaline, because over-acid soil will limit the number of species that can be grown. It is worth buying one of the soil-testing kits that are on sale at most garden centres and nurseries. These are easy to use and not expensive, and testing your soil will, in the long term, save you from wasting money on plants that will not thrive in your particular type of soil. Some plants will grow in extremely poor soil, even in sandy terrain, but if you feel that your soil needs correction, seek professional advice,

which should be available at most large garden centres or nurseries.

There is an enormous choice of flowers suitable for drying and, unless you have an exceptionally large garden, you should not attempt to grow all of them. Select types of flowers that have different shapes and textures as well as different colours, and choose species and varieties that can be picked at different times, so that you do not overcrowd your drying area. I have listed below some of the plants that can be grown and dried successfully, but there are many other flowers that will also dry well, so do experiment with whatever flowers appeal to you.

ACHILLEA
(perennial)

There are at least three types of achillea that are suitable for drying. They are fairly hardy plants and easy to grow, and all three species listed here will grow even in poor soil, as long as it is well drained.

ACHILLEA FILIPENDULINA

This plant can grow tall – sometimes over 3-4ft (0.9-1.2m). The flowers, a bright mustard yellow, are borne in very flat heads, which are formed by masses of little florets. The heads can measure up to 6in (15cm) across. This is a good plant for tall and autumnal displays, and it should be grown in full sunshine.

ACHILLEA MILLEFOLIUM

There is a white, wild variety of *A. millefolium* (yarrow) which has white flowers, and also a cultivated type called 'Cerise Queen', with flowers in varying shades of light red; other varieties can be found with pink and lilac blooms. This type of achillea bears its flowers in flat heads, not quite as large as those of *A. filipendulina*, and it does not grow as tall as that species. *A. millefolium* grows in any soil and will flower from mid-summer. It prefers a sunny position.

OPPOSITE: these larkspur, in a wonderful range of pastel colours, are ready to be harvested for drying.

ACHILLEA PTARMICA

One of the best varieties of achillea is named 'The Pearl', and this is a very good description. It has white flowers, consisting of small, pompon-like florets, and it is an excellent substitute for gypsophila in arrangements. The florets remain a good size when dried. 'The Pearl' flowers from mid-summer and grows to about 30in (75cm) high. Like the other species, it prefers a sunny position.

ACONITUM
(perennial)

Commonly called monkshood, *A. napellus* is tall and spiky, with small flowers growing up the stem. The dusky purple-blue flowers will dry to a darker blue. An attractive plant, which likes good soil and will grow to 3-4ft (0.9-1.2m), it can flower from late spring to mid-summer but needs at least 6 hours sunshine a day. Monkshood is poisonous, so it is best not to grow it if you have small children, and you should always wash your hands after handling it.

ADIANTUM
(perennial)

Usually referred to as maidenhair fern, *A. capillus-veneris* turns a wonderful deep green when dried, and it is invaluable for making bouquets and tussie-mussies. Its elegant fronds lend a refined touch to Christmas arrangements and mix brilliantly with cones and red roses. Maidenhair ferns need rich, peaty, moist soil, which should never be allowed to dry out, and they should be planted in shade. The fronds will grow to a length of about 12in (30cm).

ALCEA
(biennial)

A. rosea (syn. *Althaea rosea*) is better known as the hollyhock. This magnificent plant can grow to amazing heights, some varieties reaching 8ft (2.4m), and it should be placed at the back of a border, preferably near a wall. The flowers, which grow up the stem and can be found in many attractive colours, should be dried using silica gel. Hollyhocks prefer sunshine, although they will grow in semi-shade, and they must be kept well watered. They will flower from mid-summer to early autumn.

ALCHEMILLA
(perennial)

A. mollis, also known as lady's mantle, is a favourite in herbaceous borders, where it will spread each year. A delightful addition to any garden, the delicate, greeny-yellow flowers resemble lace, and they dry extremely well. The leaves press beautifully as well as being successful when hung to dry. Alchemillas should be planted towards the middle of the border since they grow to a maximum of 20in (50cm). They thrive in damp soil and prefer a position in semi-shade; when flowers will be produced from mid-summer until early autumn.

ALLIUM
(bulb)
ALLIUM GIGANTEUM

Often known as the decorative onion, *A. giganteum* is, as its name suggests, a very large allium, which can grow to 5ft (1.5m) tall. It produces purple flowers, which resemble balls and which can be 5in (13cm) across, from mid-summer. The bulbs should be planted in autumn, and they must be kept well watered from spring. Although it will tolerate sandy soil, *A. giganteum* is tender and requires a sheltered spot.

ALLIUM SCHOENOPRASUM

Chives (*A. schoenoprasum*) also produce pretty spherical heads that can also be dried successfully. The flowers are pinkish-purple. You can plant chives almost anywhere as they are not fussy.

AMARANTHUS
(annual)

An extraordinary looking plant, *A. caudatus*, which is usually called love-lies-bleeding, has cascades of pointed spikes, draped in clusters and hanging from the stems. Planted in full sunshine, it will flower at two- or three-week intervals from late summer onwards. There is no correct time for picking the flowers, but I would suggest gathering the spikes before they become too enormous. Amaranthus needs full sun, and, as it is quite tender, it should be given a sheltered spot.

AMMOBIUM
(annual)

Known as winged everlasting daisy or everlasting sunflower, the pretty, small daisy-type heads of *A. alatum* are very effective for arrangements, but to create any effect they must be displayed in abundance. The heads will flop if they are not supported, and they really benefit from being mixed with other flowers. Ammobiums originally came from Australia, and although they will grow in any soil, they need plenty of sunshine and a sheltered spot, when they can grow to about 3ft (90cm) tall.

ANAPHALIS
(perennial)

A. triplinervis var. *intermedia* bears extremely pretty soft, white, fluffy flowers. The leaves are also attractive, being a sort of silver-green. Anaphalis flowers in mid-summer, and grows to about 18in (45cm) tall. Ideally, it should be planted in a sunny position in well-drained soil, but it will grow in shade if you are short of space.

ANEMONE
(tuber)

There are several species of anemone, but the varieties of *A. coronaria* are especially popular for their masses of different, vivid colours. Anenomes will only dry successfully in a desiccant or if they are pressed. The colours remain bright, even after drying, and look stunning incorporated into wreaths and swags. Among the best varieties are 'The Bride', De Caen hybrids and 'Hollandia', which are all spring-flowering. You can also obtain other species to grow for summer and autumn flowers if you wish. Anenomes need good, well-drained soil and will grow to a maximum height of 12in (30cm). *A. coronaria* and its varieties prefer a position in full sun.

ARTEMISIA
(perennial)

This cheerful group of herbs, commonly called wormwood, is often dried for its wonderful aroma, but the silvery grey-green foliage is also beautiful when dried; the flowers are of little interest. The leaves are a very unusual colour, which will mix perfectly with soft pastel shades of pinks, lilacs and blues. *A. ludoviciana*, which is sometimes known as white sage, likes to be in full sunlight in a well-drained spot, where it will grow to about 3ft (90cm), while 'Lambrook Silver', a variety of *A. absinthium*, is one to look out for; it can grow to a height of about 30in (75cm). Probably the best, however, is *A. schmidtiana*, with its fine-spun silver foliage. The variety *A. schmidtiana* 'Nana' grows to only 2-4in (5-10cm) tall and is delightful. Artemisias flower throughout the summer. Tarragon is also a type of artemisia, *A. dranunculus*, but I find the leaves of no use since they become too brittle when hung dried, although they can be pressed successfully.

ASTILBE × ARENDSII
(perennial)

Astilbes are among the prettiest of plants, bearing feathery plumes of varying shades of pink and red. They like to be near water, and the soil must be kept moist at all times. You can plant astilbes in semi-shade, as they do not enjoy very hot weather, and in rich earth they will reach heights over 3ft (90cm). They flower in mid-summer.

BRIZA
(annual)

This plant is known as quaking grass, and its appearance fits its name, the little heads bobbing and bending with the slightest breeze. Since most dried flowers appear to be rather stiff, briza brings a welcome contrast and can be added to displays to give an impression of movement. Briza turns a delicate green as it grows and is best picked at that moment, usually in mid-summer, when the ears have formed but not opened. *B. media* (common quaking grass) will grow to about 15in (38cm), and *B. maxima* (greater quaking grass) will attain a height of 20in (50cm), but both species like ordinary soil and will benefit from lots of sunshine.

CELOSIA
(annual)

Often known as cockscomb, *C. cristata* certainly lives up to its name. It has bright red plumage that resembles wattles! This is an easy plant to dry, but care must be taken over it in the garden. The most popular type for use as a dried subject is the scarlet variety 'Coral Garden'. Celosias do not grow very tall, to approximately 10in (25cm), and they require very rich, moist soil and a sunny position, when they will flower from mid-summer.

CHRYSANTHEMUM
(annual and perennial)

Chrysanthemums, which traditionally flower in autumn, are most useful for adding colour to your supplies if you find that you have not been successful with some of your summer drying. All types require fairly rich, moist soil, and they like to be grown in sunshine. It is possible to find chrysanthemums that will grow from 4in (10cm) to more than 4ft (1.2m) in the right conditions. Both the single, daisy-shaped varieties and the multi-petalled, pompon types will dry nicely, and they can either be hung dried or dried in silica gel.

DELPHINIUM
(perennial and annual)

Delphiniums and larkspur, which are members of the same family, are two magnificent plants, and no garden is complete without them. Most delphiniums are perennial, although there are some annual species, whereas larkspur are annuals. Many of the favourite varieties are in stunning shades of blue and pink, but some are now available in creams and yellows as well. The large delphiniums can grow to a maximum of 5ft (1.5m), while larkspur are shorter, although they, too, may reach 4ft (1.2m). All varieties of both plants must be placed at the back of a fenced or walled border or in the middle of a central bed, and they will probably have to be staked if they are in an unprotected site. They need lots of sun and well-drained, rich soil. Both delphiniums and larkspur flower from early summer onwards, and they may produce a second flush of flowers in autumn.

DIANTHUS
(annual and perennial)

Pinks and carnations need little looking after once they are established in the garden. Care must be taken to ensure that the soil is lime based and always kept moist, although it must be free draining. Dianthus need the sun and, depending on variety, will grow from 6in (15cm) to over 2ft (60cm). Flowers are borne from late spring to mid-summer, and some of the repeat-flowering varieties produce a second flush. The flowers can be air dried, flat dried or dried using silica gel, each method producing a different result but, unfortunately, the blooms lose their wonderful scent when dried.

ECHINOPS
(perennial)

Echinops ritro is a magnificent plant with steely blue, globular, thistle-like heads. The flowers look wonderful in mixed arrangements, their shape being quite different from that of other plants. Although they do not need much care while growing, they do not like soggy earth – the soil can be ordinary but it must be well drained – and they prefer a sunny position. They will grow from 2ft (60cm) to 5ft (1.5m) or more high, and the spiky flower heads are produced in mid-summer.

ERYNGIUM
(perennial)

Eryingium, which is usually called sea holly, is a thistle-like plant, and its steely blue flowers are rather prickly but extremely useful for arranging as blue flowers are few. Sea holly does not change colour when it dries, but it is quite green in its early stages, so wait until the flower heads have developed into a good blue before picking them. There are three species to grow: *E. alpinum*, *E. maritimum*, which is the true native English sea holly, and *E. x oliverianum*. The species range in size from 12in (30cm) to 3ft (90cm). Sea holly

should be grown in a sunny position in well-drained, ordinary soil. The plants need little attention and will flower from mid-summer to autumn.

FILIPENDULA
(perennial)

F. ulmaria is known as meadowsweet, and it is such a pretty flower, which can be found growing wild in the countryside, along ditches and in wet meadows. As you can tell, it likes water and, if you grow one of the cultivated varieties in the garden, it must be kept moist at all times. The wild species is white, but there are several cultivars with coloured blooms, and *F. rubra* has pink flowers. The flowers have a romantic appeal, from a distance resembling fluffy cotton wool. The seed heads are also excellent in dried-flower bouquets. Meadowsweet, which grows to about 36in (90cm), likes ordinary soil and semi-shade, and the flowers are borne from early to mid-summer.

GOMPHRENA
(annual, biennial, perennial)

Only one species of gomphrena, *G. globosa*, is in general cultivation. Its flowers resemble clover and they are available in shades of yellow, pink, lilac and orange. There is also a white variety, which I find rather dull when dried. Gomphrena, which is sometimes known as the globe amaranth, must be grown in a sunny position and have plenty of water. The plants grow approximately 12in (30cm) tall and prefer ordinary soil. Flowers are borne in summer and early autumn.

GYPSOPHILA
(annual, perennial)

A favourite with many, many people and a must for dried-flower enthusiasts, gypsophila looks beautiful while growing and is just as attractive when dried. It creates a wonderful haze around all the other flowers and is perfect for incorporating into wedding bouquets. There are several species, but only two are widely cultivated. *G. elegans*, an annual, has clusters of tiny, white flowers borne on branching stems, and *G. paniculata*, which is a perennial and the more common, has fluffy white bobbles, resembling a snow storm, borne on wiry stems. A smaller variety, *G. paniculata* 'Album', is a tiny-headed form that dries particularly well. Gypsophila needs full sunshine and not too much watering. Both species grow from 12in (30cm) to 4ft (1.2m), and they prefer rich, light soil. The flowers appear from late summer to early autumn. If you are not successful with your crop, it is widely available from florists during the summer months.

Summer flowers surround this mist of gypsophila.

HELIPTERUM
(annual)
HELIPTERUM MANGLESII
(syn. *Rhodanthe manglesii*)

The rhodanthe daisy, as *H. manglesii* is sometimes known, is an extremely pretty flower. The blooms can be pink or white, and they have delicate yellow centres. Many people are put off drying this daisy since it sheds its petals while it is being arranged, but I find it invaluable, and a gentle coating of hair-spray usually sorts the problem out. Rhodanthes look best on their own in hugh masses, and they make stunning fireplace displays. The plants like any soil and seem to thrive if there is a sandy base, when they grow to about 12in (30cm). Flowers appear from mid-summer.

HELIPTERUM ROSEUM
(syn. *Acroclinium roseum*)
(annual)

This plant has a large, daisy-shaped flower, which is perfect for drying, and when dried, its appearance is very similar to the large marguerite daisy. Garden daisies do not dry well, nor even press well, so helipterums are extremely useful in arrangements that require a daisy-like shape. They are charming massed in a vase on their own or mixed with other flowers and grasses to form country-style displays. The flowers can be found in pink or white, both with yellow centres, and there is another variety, 'Red Bonnie', which has far deeper pink flowers with black centres. All varieties require ordinary or even sandy soil and plenty of sunshine, and they will flower from mid-summer.

HYDRANGEA
(deciduous shrub)

This is such a pleasing flower to both grow and dry. Throughout the summer months the vast bushes provide huge splashes of colour, ranging from white to incredible shades of pink, blue and lilac, and some of the lacecap hydrangeas can appear to be almost green. This is one of the most useful flowers for large displays, as it looks stunning on its own as well as giving bulk to any arrangement. The petals can be pressed brilliantly or they can be used for decorating bowls of pot pourri. *H. macrophylla* is the most widely available species, and there are many named varieties to choose from. Bushes need several years to produce quantities of blooms, but this is well worth the investment. The colour of the flowers depends on the type of soil, acid soils producing blue flowers, and alkaline soil pink blooms. All hydrangeas, however, prefer rich, well-drained soil and to be grown in semi-shade. They can grow to enormous heights, sometimes up to 10ft (3m) in the right conditions, but 5-6ft (1.5-1.8m) is more usual.

An English country garden in mid-summer, with 'Hidcote' lavender providing the stunning borders.

LANTANA
(annual)

The main problem with *L. camara* is that it is very prone to attack by insects, and you will have to use insecticides to protect it from both red spider mite and whitefly. Tiny flowers, which open yellow and turn red, are borne in dense heads throughout summer, and in the autumn these give way to attractive pods, which dry easily and are an interesting shape for dried-flower displays. Lantana is tender and should be grown in full sun in rich, well-drained soil. In a sheltered spot it will grow to about 5ft (1.5m).

LAVANDULA
(perennial)

No garden is complete without a lavender bush, and the uses to which this wonderfully perfumed plant can be put are almost endless. Lavender dries beautifully and remains fragrant. *L. angustifolia* (syn. *L. spica*) is, I think, the prettiest species, with its pale grey-blue florets, and it is wonderful for making into lavender bottles (see page 148). Try growing the variety 'Hidcote', which has very dark blue flowers and a rich perfume. Lavender thrives in ordinary soil and loves the sun. Established bushes can grow to 4ft (1.2m), and the flowers attract a wonderful array of bees and butterflies.

LIMONIUM
(perennial)

Sea lavender, or statice as it is often known, is an excellent filler for dried-flower displays. There are two main species to grow – *L. latifolium* and *L. sinuatum*. *L. latifolium* is the softer and more flexible plant of the two; try the variety 'Caspia' – its stems, which can grow to 2ft (60cm), dry beautifully. The little flowers, which are borne in dense sprays, are a delicate blue while they are growing but become virtually white when dried. *L. sinuatum* is, perhaps, the best known member of the family and was probably the original dried flower! It is a more upright, bushy plant than *L. latifolium* and grows to about 18in (45cm). The tiny flowers, which are available in brilliant shades of purple, pink, yellow and peach, are borne in clusters on the stems and dry before you have time to harvest them. *L. tartaricum*, which is smaller and bears pale pink flowers, is widely used in dried-flower arranging. All species will thrive in ordinary soil, even if you live near to the sea, but they do need to be kept well watered and to be grown in a sunny spot. The flowers appear in mid-summer and last until early autumn. If you cannot manage to grow limonium in your garden, I would suggest that you obtain some from your florist as it is an invaluable addition to many types of arrangement.

LONAS
(annual)

L. indorra has mustard yellow, bobbly florets, which grow in clusters to form a rather flat head. It is a very useful flower for dried-flower decorations and is a good substitute when *Achillea filipendulina* is not available. Lonas grows easily in ordinary, rather sandy soil, but it prefers a sunny position. The stems will grow to 12-15in (30-38cm), and flowers are borne in mid-summer.

LUNARIA
(biennial)

Better known as honesty, *L. annua* will grow anywhere, and once it takes a hold, you will have it in your garden forever! Honesty will grow in sun although it prefers semi-shade, and it produces purple flowers from late spring to early summer. Of more interest than the blooms in dried-flower arrangements, however, are the circular, flat, green pods, which dry out indoors to reveal silver interiors. Honesty can grow very tall, up to at least 36in (90cm), and a bunch of the silvery, transparent seed heads will look stunning placed in a vase on their own.

MOLUCELLA
(annual)

M. laevis is commonly called bells of Ireland, and this beautiful plant resembles its name. Its other common name is shell-flower, and its long stems are covered from top to bottom in exquisite bell-shaped leaves. This is not an easy plant to dry, but it is well worth trying. Some years I have had great success with it. Molucella should be planted in a sunny position, and, as it grows quite tall, 2-3ft (60-90cm), it should be placed towards the back of the border. It will do best in rich, well-drained soil, and the flowers are borne in mid-summer.

NARCISSUS
(bulb)

Narcissi, or daffodils as we know them better, flower in spring, and they are one of the earliest plants to appear. There are many different varieties to cultivate, and your choice will depend on personal taste, garden space and requirements. It would be sensible to look at the coloured brochures produced by garden centres and nurseries or seek professional advice. Both the single and multi-petalled varieties are suitable for drying and pressing. They can be dried using silica gel and look stunning in Easter displays (see page 56). Daffodils will grow to heights ranging from 6 to 20in (15-50cm), and they can be planted in banks and borders or naturalized in grass; they will also flourish in semi-shade under trees. Plant the bulbs in autumn in well-drained but moist soil and leave them undisturbed.

A brilliant array of garden flowers – love-in-a-mist, delphiniums, cranesbill and little yellow Welsh poppies – grown for drying, pressing and use in pot pourri.

NIGELLA
(annual)

You will know *N. damascena* as love-in-a-mist, and the name describes it perfectly. The pale blue, pink or white flowers sit in a fine cobweb of foliage, just as if they really were being seen through a hazy mist. Planted *en masse*, they can make a wonderful splash of colour. There are two ways to enjoy this plant for drying. You can pick it when the pastel blooms appear, or you can wait until flowering is over, when the fairly large, stripy pods appear. Both flowers and pods dry well, and I would take advantage of the flowers to add blue material to your dried stores. Nigella prefers to be grown in sun, and it will thrive in any rich, well-drained soil. The plants will grow to approximately 24in (60cm), and flowers appear throughout summer.

PÆONIA
(deciduous shrub)

Peony shrubs flower so briefly that you cannot feel guilty about picking and drying as many of the blooms as possible. There are dozens of varieties to choose from, but I would recommend that you grow three colours – one white, one pink and one crimson variety. This will give you all the scope you need for arranging. The multi-petalled, double varieties look the most impressive when dried, and you should look out for *P. officinalis* 'Rubra Plena', which has magenta flowers, 'Rosea Plena', which produces pink blooms, and 'Madame Calot', which has pale pink blooms that eventually turn white. Peonies like to be kept well watered and prefer sun, although they will tolerate semi-shade. Once established, bushes can grow up to about 4ft (1.2m). Most peonies flower in early summer, and the blooms can be dried by hanging or by using a desiccant such as silica gel.

PHYSALIS
(perennial)

P. alkekengi or Chinese lanterns produce glorious orange pods, which are ready to be harvested in autumn and can very easily be air dried. Keep the foliage on the stems as they can look rather bare without it. Once it is established in your garden, this plant can literally take over, so try planting it near to a path where it will not be able to spread. Physalis grows in any well-drained soil to a height of about 2ft (60cm), and it will thrive in a sunny spot.

PSYLLIOSTACHYS
(annual)

P. suworowii (syn. *Statice suworowii*) is often called pink poker, and its name is very apt. Minute, pinky-mauve florets are borne on spiky, branching stems, which are about 18in (45cm) long. The flower spikes dry extremely well. Pink poker will thrive in ordinary, well-drained, even sandy, soil but requires plenty of sun. The flowers are produced in summer and early autumn.

ROSA
(shrub)

There are so many types of rose that it would be impossible to list them all – they would make a book on their own! Roses are thought of as romantic flowers, and they are, of course, simply wonderful in any garden, but they are also fragrant and beautiful additions to dried-flower arrangements. Hybrid Tea roses (large-flowered bush roses) are the most suitable for drying, but it is best to avoid single varieties or any rose with lax petals, which seem to drop off while drying. Some to try are 'Red Devil', the yellow 'Golden Times' or the pink 'Eden Rose' and 'Fragrant Cloud'. I have had great success drying all types of old fashioned roses, but they must be picked before they are in full bloom: the bud should just be opening to reveal the petals inside. Silica gel is useful for drying larger roses, and they can then be used for garlands and for decorating pot pourri. Because there are so many different varieties to choose from, it is worthwhile trying to obtain advice from your local nursery on which ones will suit your soil type. Roses will flower throughout summer and in to early autumn.

Hazy gypsophila is the perfect complement for this vivid red rose and buds.

SALVIA
(annual, perennial)

There are two species of salvia that are suitable for drying: *S. horminum*, which is an annual, and the perennial *S. x superba*. *S. x superba* can be an excellent replacement for lavender; it is the same shape, but has rather deeper blue flowers. Both species like ordinary, well-drained soil and a sunny position. *S. horminum*, which has white or pink to deep purple flowers, will grow to 9-18in (23-45cm) high, while *S. x superba* can reach 2ft (60cm) or more.

SANTOLINA
(perennial)

This is usually called cotton lavender, and its silver-grey foliage and yellow button heads are outstanding. The heads dry beautifully and retain their shape, and it is a fragrant plant, often used in pot pourri. Santolinas will grow in ordinary soil, preferring stone walls and crannies to grow in, and they require plenty of sunshine. There are several cultivars to choose from, ranging in height from 1ft 6in to 3ft (45-90cm). The flowers are produced in mid- to late summer.

SILENE
(perennial)

Sometimes called campion or catchfly, silene produces pretty, delicate, pink flowers that appear in mid-summer. The flowers are rather fragile, but they are perfect for small bouquets or when arranged *en masse*. Grow silene in the sun in ordinary, light soil. It will grow to about 18in (45cm). *S. casinianum* is available in specialist shops.

SOLIDAGO
(perennial)

The brilliant yellow flowers of golden rod appear in late summer. The plant can be picked while the flower panicles are still green or they can be left until they turn yellow, giving you a variety of colours for drying. One of the most popular species is *S. canadensis*, and there are several varieties available, which can grow up to 6ft (1.8m). Solidago will grow in semi-shade or in sun in any well-drained soil, and once it is established will flower year after year.

STACHYS
(perennial)

Stachys, which is widely known as bunnies' ears or lamb's tongue, has unusual, soft grey-green foliage and produces tiny pink flowers, which grow at the end of long stems. The leaves have a woolly appearance and dry well, giving both an unusual shape and texture in your displays. *S. byzantina* (syn. *S. lanata*) can be grown in ordinary, even poor, soil, but it must be kept well drained. The plants are 12-15in (30-38cm) high, and the rather insignificant flowers appear throughout summer. They are excellent plants for the front of the border.

TAGETES
(annual)

Marigolds are such useful plants in the garden, providing a splash of colour at the front of the border throughout the summer. The fat, multi-petalled heads will dry well, too, forming a pretty orange ball, and they are useful in pot pourri. Plant marigolds in groups on their own, since their strident colours will clash with many other plants, although they do look most attractive planted near artemisias. Depending on the variety selected, marigolds will grow from 8 to 30in (20-90cm). All cultivars will be happy in ordinary soil, but they do like plenty of sunshine. The flowers are produced from mid-summer until the first frosts. Don't forget that marigold petals are a colourful, nutritious and tasty addition to salads.

TULIPA
(bulb)

I have not had much success with air drying tulips, which seem to dry well only in silica gel. They can, however, be flat dried, and their petals used for pot pourri. Plant the bulbs in autumn, for spring flowering. There are many different shades available, and any of the colours will dry beautifully. Tulips should be kept moist and they need plenty of sun. There are dozens of varieties to choose from, ranging in height from less than 6in (15cm) to over 2ft (60cm).

ZINNIA
(annual, perennial)

Zinnias make excellent dried flowers, and they are easy to grow. The colours are brilliant, and if you dead-head regularly, you will obtain masses of blooms. The multi-petalled species *Z. elegans* is the best to grow for drying, and the flower heads form balls when dried. Plant in ordinary, well-drained soil in a sunny spot. Zinnias grow to 24-36in (60-90cm) and flower from mid-summer to early autumn.

OPPOSITE: climbing roses are seen to best effect against old garden walls.

HARVESTING YOUR FLOWERS

After all your hard work in the garden during the summer months, harvesting your flowers must be done with loving care! Most flowers are best picked a few days before they reach their prime, and some should be harvested earlier, just before the buds burst open. Not all flowers will be ready at the same time, and each year, of course, the timing will depend on the weather conditions: some years a flower that is normally ready to be picked in June, will be ready in July or even May.

As your plants reach flowering point you will need to inspect them each day, as a sudden shower of rain or a morning of hot sunshine can alter them so quickly. It is fun to experiment by picking the same variety of flower at different stages so that you have as many shapes as possible. If a flower opens too widely to be suitable for air drying, try using a desiccant instead. For the first few years your growing and harvesting will be largely experimental, but you will quickly become knowledgeable about what to grow and when to pick.

Flowers should be harvested when they are completely dry; never pick them after rain or if they are laden with dew. Mid-morning is usually the best time, as often, by the afternoon, flowers will have begun to wilt slightly and need moisture to revive them. Pick only the most perfect blooms, as damaged flowers and leaves will look unsightly when dried, and flowers that have gone over will often just drop while they are drying.

Having prepared the area where your flowers will dry (see the next chapter), you will require certain materials to look after them while you prepare the bunches.

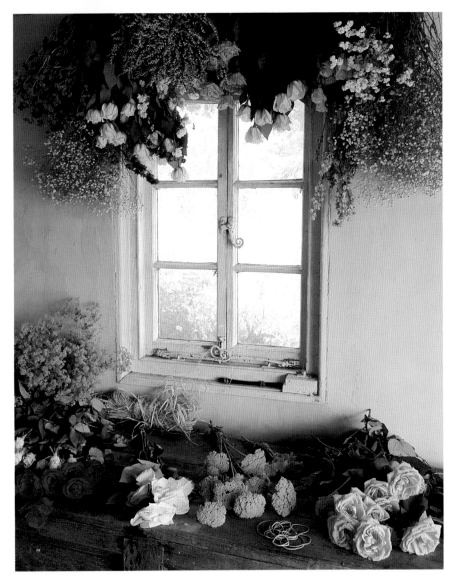

YOU WILL NEED

Secateurs (clippers)

Strong scissors

A large trug or flower basket

Several large containers filled with water

Never attempt to harvest too many flowers at once. Preparing for drying takes time, and you may find that you cannot complete this stage if you have too many blooms. Pick the flowers at the very base of the stem to maximize the lengths available for arranging and lay them carefully in a garden trug or flower-picking basket. Never place too many in the trug at once, or you will damage the ones below. In addition, it is advisable to harvest only one type of flower at a time. Stems seem to get tangled around each other of their own accord, and you will find your work is far harder if you pick, say, roses with all their prickles at the same time as gypsophila, which seems to cling to everything around it.

If it is a very warm day, prepare some containers with enough water in the bottom to give the flowers a drink while you are preparing others for drying. Have a table ready to sort the flowers into bunches, a task that is best done outside.

There are no pre-arranged times for harvesting, but the list on page 24 is a guide to work from.

Freshly picked flowers being sorted into small bunches for air drying.

OPPOSITE: a garden gazebo is an ideal place to hang flowers to dry.

WHEN TO PICK AND HOW TO DRY YOUR FLOWERS

FLOWER	PICK	METHOD	DRYING TIME
Achillea	Full bloom	Air dry	4-7 days
Aconitum	Semi-/full bloom	Air dry	3-5 days
Adiantum	Full bloom	Air dry	2-4 days
Alcea	Full bloom	Desiccant	3-4 days
Alchemilla	Full bloom	Air dry	3-5 days
Allium	Full bloom	Air dry	5-7 days
Amaranthus	Tight bloom	Air dry	4-6 days
Ammobium	Semi-/full bloom	Air dry	3-5 days
Anaphalis	Full bloom	Air dry	3-5 days
Anemone	Semi-/full bloom	Desiccant	2-3 days
Artemisia	Bud/full bloom	Air dry	2-4 days
Astilbe	Full bloom	Air dry	3-5 days
Briza	When green	Air dry	2-4 days
Celosia	Full bloom	Air dry	4-7 days
Chrysanthemum	Semi-/full bloom	Desiccant	3-4 days
Delphinium	Semi-/full bloom	Air dry/desiccant	5/3 days
Dianthus	Full bloom	Desiccant	3-4 days
Echinops	When blue	Air dry	4-5 days
Eryngium	Full blue bloom	Air dry	3-5 days
Filipendula	Full bloom	Air dry/desiccant	4/3 days
Gomphrena	Full bloom	Air dry	3-4 days
Gypsophila	Full bloom	Air dry/glycerine	3/8 days
Helichrysum	Semi-open	Air dry	3-4 days
Helipterum	Full bloom	Air dry	3-5 days
Hydrangea	Full bloom (late September)	Water dry	4-7 days
Lantana	When pods appear	Air dry	3-5 days
Lavandula	Full bloom	Air dry	3-4 days
Limonium	Full bloom	Air dry	3-4 days
Lonas	Full bloom	Air dry	3-5 days
Lunaria	When pods turn brown	Air dry	2-4 days
Molucella	Full bloom	Air dry/glycerine	8/10 days
Narcissus	Full bloom	Desiccant	3-4 days
Nigella	Full bloom and pods	Air dry	3-5 days
Paeonia	Open bud/full bloom	Air dry/desiccant	5/5 days
Physalis	Orange pod	Air dry	3-5 days
Psylliostachys	Full bloom	Air dry	3-5 days
Rosa	Open bud/full bloom	Air dry/desiccant	5/4 days
Salvia	Semi-/full bloom	Air dry	3-5 days
Santolina	Bud/full bloom	Air dry	3-7 days
Silene	Full bloom	Air dry	3-4 days
Solidago	Green/yellow bloom	Air dry	3-6 days
Stachys	Full bloom	Air dry	4-6 days
Tagetes	Full bloom	Air dry/desiccant	5/4 days
Tulipa	Semi-bloom	Desiccant	3-4 days
Zinnia	Full bloom	Air dry/desiccant	5/4 days

Air-drying times vary enormously depending on the conditions. If the weather is wonderfully warm and there is not too much damp in the air, the flowers may dry more quickly than indicated here; if it is humid or rather cold, the flowers will take longer to dry.

Many of the flowers listed here may be picked when in bud as well as in full bloom, which will give you a wider variety of shapes to include in your arrangements. Generally, most flowers should be picked at their peak, just before they reach overtly wide bloom, but solidago, for example, is very pretty in its green bud stage and delightful when the yellow flowers begin to appear. Nigella can be picked both for the wonderful blue flowers and for the stripy seed pods. It is also possible to press many of these garden flowers successfully, and this is discussed on pages 88-9.

Bunches of garden flowers hung to air dry.

PAGES 26-7: rose heads that have been dried in silica gel.

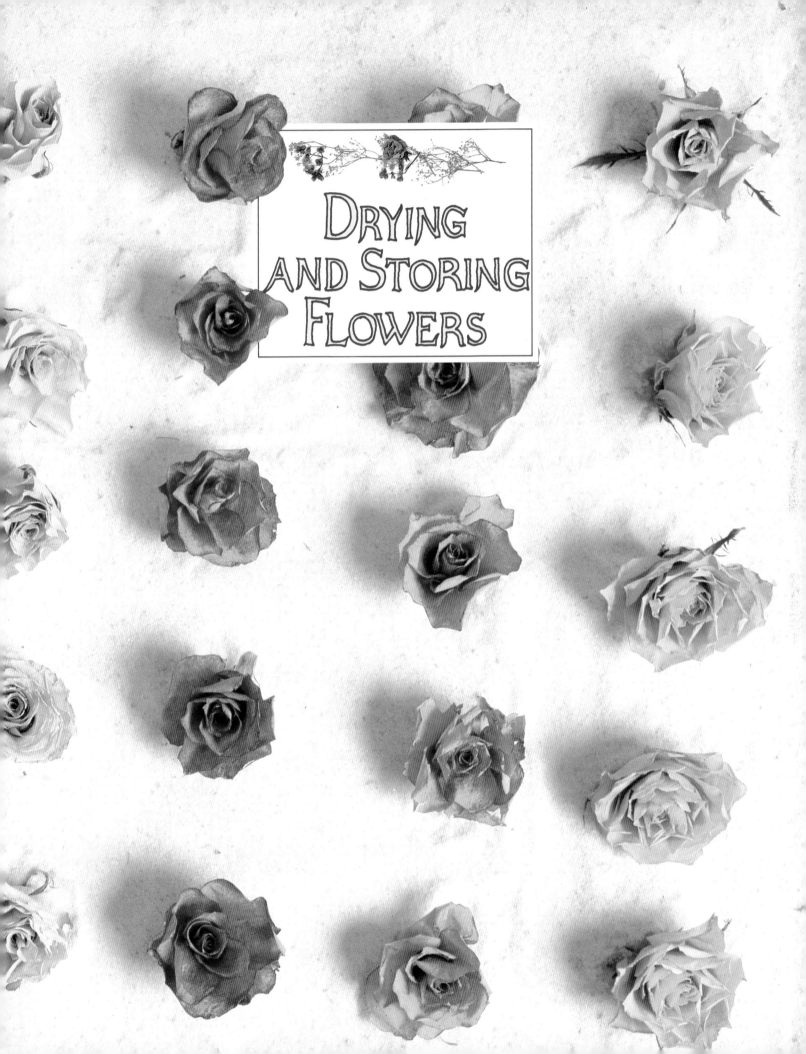

DRYING
AND STORING
FLOWERS

HOW TO DRY FLOWERS

Drying flowers is a rewarding occupation and a delightful way to preserve the beautiful flowers from your garden. It is a time-consuming process, but your efforts will be rewarded by having flowers in your home throughout the long winter months when fresh flowers become rather expensive to buy and the choice is limited.

There are three rules to observe if you are going to dry flowers from your garden successfully every time. First, you must ensure that the quality of the flowers is of the highest possible standard. They must be free of blight or blemish, so choose only the most perfect blooms. A petal that has already started to wither or to turn brown will simply shrivel and become even browner when it is dried.

Second, the flowers that you are preparing for drying must be absolutely dry. Make sure there are no dew or rain drops on them, or the petals will go mouldy and rot. In an emergency – if it has been raining for days, and the flowers are ready for drying, for example – pick them and place them in a vase overnight to dry off.

Third, the place you select to dry the flowers must be completely free from damp. Anywhere spacious and warm, away from direct light, is suitable, but a completely dark area would be ideal. Wherever you choose, there should always be air circulating. The best areas are large, walk-in cupboards, storerooms, outhouses or large lofts. You can use your kitchen if there is a beam from which you can suspend your blooms, but make sure that it is not immediately above a working area such as the sink or cooker, where the flowers would be damaged by steam.

There are various methods of drying your flowers, each producing a different type of result. The simplest way is air drying, in which the flowers are hung in rows from a wire and allowed to dry naturally. You can also dry by using a desiccant, a substance such as silica gel or sand. Some flowers, such as those with huge daisy heads or sun flowers, should be dried flat, while using glycerine for stems of leaves, including all the broad-leaved types like beech, oak, bay and pittosporum, gives the most satisfactory results. For emergency drying, you can try your oven or microwave, set at a very low temperature, and this can be especially useful for drying individual petals or flower heads. There are a few types of flowers that will dry better if they are stood in just enough water to cover the last inch of the stem; this method is particularly suitable for hydrangeas.

AIR DRYING BY HANGING

Air drying is the easiest method, and it is ideal for bulk drying large quantities of garden flowers, especially long-stemmed varieties destined for larger displays. The secret is to try to dry the flowers as quickly as possible in order to retain their colours.

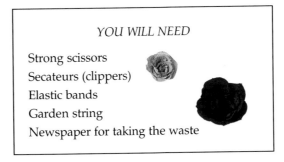

YOU WILL NEED

Strong scissors
Secateurs (clippers)
Elastic bands
Garden string
Newspaper for taking the waste

The first step is to take the stems, one by one, and strip off any unwanted leaves. Most varieties benefit from this, as it means that they retain less moisture so that the drying process is quicker. Flowers such as roses, carthamus (dyer's saffron), wheat, alchemilla and achillea 'The Pearl' often look better with the top leaves left on as they can seem rather bare without them. With such plants, strip off only small leaves that are close to the stem. Alchemilla leaves can be dried separately, as can peony leaves, but they do tend to become rather brittle when dried, so great care is needed when arranging them.

Do not be tempted to bunch too many flowers together, and make sure that the flower heads are not closely touching each other. Five or six heads placed in different positions are best (see opposite). Some very large heads, such as peony flowers, can even be dried individually. Remember, the closer together the flowers are, the longer they will take to dry. Spiky stems, such as larkspur, delphiniums or monkshood, should be dried in bunches of six or eight stems. Use an elastic band to bunch the flowers, because this allows for stem shrinkage. Flower stems tied with string may slip out while they are drying. Make sure that

OPPOSITE: dried flowers ready to be sorted before they are stored.

An arrangement of summer flowers – peonies, tulips and larkspur – that were dried using the desiccant silica gel.

the flowers are not tangled when you bunch them, as they will dry in that position and be difficult to disentangle.

Hang the bunched flowers from a wire or string suspended between hooks that have been extremely well secured into the ceiling. A large number of bunches will be heavy when hung, so the hooks and wire must be strong. If you have a special outhouse, which can be used over and over again for this purpose, you could try suspending a large expanse of wire netting just below the ceiling. This is an ideal way of supporting the flowers and leaves plenty of room for air to circulate.

Drying can take anything from a few days to several weeks, depending on the size of the flowers and the temperature of the place in which you dry them. Check the flowers from time to time. They will feel quite crisp when they are ready. Feel large-headed flowers just at the base of the flower head, pinching in very gently to check for any dampness.

DRYING WITH SILICA GEL

Drying flowers in a desiccant is a totally different process from air drying, and the results can be spectacular, the flowers often appearing almost fresh and retaining their colours beautifully. Roses, hollyhock florets, rhododendrons, lilac heads, peonies, hydrangeas, daffodils, tulips and many others will practically retain their natural shapes.

Silica gel, the easiest and quickest desiccant to use, is available from most chemists. It resembles preserving sugar or rock salt, and the granules must be ground down until they are as fine as castor sugar. You can buy silica gel in two forms. White granules can be bought already ground, and there is also a type that is coloured blue and that turns pink when the moisture has been absorbed and the flowers are ready. Silica gel is not cheap, but it may be reused countless times. However, if you are drying large amounts of flowers, it is advisable after much use to place the powder on a baking tray in a low oven to dry it out completely before using it again. Leave small quantities in the oven for about 30 minutes, while larger amounts will require about an hour. Set the oven at the lowest possible temperature. Do not dry silica gel in a microwave oven.

YOU WILL NEED

Airtight containers (cake tins are perfect)

Egg cartons

Small plastic flowerpots

Tape

Thin stubb wires

Strong scissors

A fine watercolour paint brush

A small spoon

Silica gel (or fine sand)

Check that the flower heads are completely dry. If you want the flowers to be wired, now is the time to do this, as it is virtually impossible to achieve once the heads are dry (see pages 46-7). Glue is the best way of securing unwired flowers.

Egg boxes are ideal if you are drying roses or flower heads that need some sort of support if they are to retain their shape. If the heads are very large, a small plastic flowerpot will work just as well, but remember, if you do use a flowerpot, to tape the bottom to cover the hole before you begin. Tins can be used for large quantities and for bigger blooms such as sprays of lilac.

Using a spoon, fill each pot or space in the egg carton to about one-third with silica gel. Place the flower head in the silica gel so that the stalk, which should have been cut just below the calyx, just touches the bottom. If the flower has been wired, cut the wire quite short (it can be added to when the flower is dry), then bend it to stick up towards the lid. Starting with the outer petals and working into the centre of the flower, spoon the silica gel between each petal, making sure that no petals are missed. The sides of the egg carton or flowerpot will take the weight of the sides of the flower, preventing it from becoming flat and losing its natural form. Keep adding the powder until the head is completely covered. Replace the lid of the egg carton or

cover the pot. Check the flowers after 48 hours to see if they are ready. Some of the larger flowers will take four or five days. Do not leave the flowers in the silica gel once the blooms are dry or they will become very crisp and disintegrate. The table below lists approximate drying times. However, these figures are only a guide, and your own experiments will quickly give you an accurate indication of the optimum times.

SMALL FLOWERS	LARGE-HEADED FLOWERS
48 hours	*up to 5 days*
Anenomes	Asters
Alstroemeria	Carnations
Bluebells	Hollyhocks
Crocus	Hydrangea
Primroses	Lilies
Tulips	Peonies
Violets	Roses

You must be extremely gentle when you remove the flower from its container; if you dig in with the spoon, you wll break the petals. Remove the top layer of silica gel with extreme caution, then, when the petals begin to appear, place the spoon down the side and lift the flower out of the container, tipping the powder back into the egg carton as you do so. Blow off the excess or use a very fine watercolour brush to remove any vestiges of the powder. A tiny spray of wax polish will revive the colour, and, if the flower feels rather frail, glue the base around the stalk to stop the petals falling away.

Store the flowers in a cardboard box with a layer of silica gel in the bottom to prevent them becoming damp.

DRYING FLAT

Drying flowers flat is a successful method for large, daisy-type flowers – for example, sunflowers – and also for roses, peonies and other types that you want to use to decorate pot pourri. Curiously, this method is not successful with flowers like pansies that are already flat; they will simply shrivel.

The flowers can either be laid on a tray or they can be placed on a wire garden sieve, their stems suspended through the mesh. The stems should be cut fairly short, and, if you wish to use them for displays, wires inserted. A garden sieve is best for this method, since you can rest it on two raised objects so that the wires have enough space beneath. If you find that the flowers fall through the mesh, bend the wires slightly below the stem, so that they hang at an angle. Flowers dried in this way will take anything from two to five days to be ready.

OVEN DRYING

This is usually a method to be used in emergencies only, and it can be very helpful if you have flowers that need drying quickly, particularly if you are short of hanging space. Many flowers can be dried well in the oven, although you will obviously have to trim the stems to fit into your oven if you want to dry the whole plant. If you are going to use a microwave oven, on no account place any wires in the flowers; this will have to be done afterwards. Drying the individual heads is preferable; it will be less complicated, and you will obtain better results. Set a conventional oven at the very lowest temperature and, if possible, leave the door slightly ajar. Small flowers will take about 30 minutes, and larger ones about an hour. Petals on their own dry quickly, and you should check every 15 minutes to see if they are ready. Microwave ovens should also be set very low; try one minute at a time.

PRESERVING WITH GLYCERINE

Glycerine is the perfect substance for preserving leaves and plants such as molucella, gypsophila and mimosa. It is also useful for some types of stems with blossoms, but this is a largely a matter of experimentation.

YOU WILL NEED

A bottle of glycerine
(available at chemists)

A large jam jar

A bucket

Salt

Strong scissors or secateurs (clippers)

Hot water

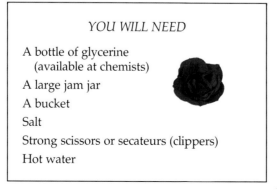

Prepare the stems before preserving by stripping all the lower part so that the leaves are not actually immersed in the liquid. The end of the stems should be flattened or split, and any unattractive upper foliage, such as torn or discoloured leaves, should be removed.

Boil approximately 2 pints (1 litre) of water and add a large tablespoon of salt. Larger quantities require the same proportion of salt to water. When the salt has dissolved and the water has cooled slightly, pour the liquid into the jar and then stand the jar in a bucket to support the leaves, which do become rather heavy and tend to topple over if unsupported. Stand the stems in the hot water and leave them for 24 hours. After that time, add one part glycerine to two parts hot water, and mix well. Empty the salty water out of the jar, and replace it with the glycerine and water, returning the jar to the bucket. Again, the stems should be immersed while the water is hot so that the mixture can reach the very top leaves and be more evenly distributed. The leaves will take anything up to 10 days to be ready. They will look darker and be slightly sticky when they are ready. Do not leave them standing in glycerine longer than necessary or the stalks will rot. Stand them in an empty jar to dry off.

The stems should not be placed in water again, and it is advisable to keep the arrangement away from a hot radiator as the leaves will begin to shrivel if they are exposed to too much heat. The perfect place for them is in an arrangement that will stand in a fireplace or in any other area that has a certain amount of freely moving air.

DRYING BY STANDING IN WATER

This method is excellent for hydrangeas, which do not always dry by hanging upside down. The florets tend to shrivel, and the wide head takes on a different shape. Gypsophila can also be dried in this way – as can many other flowers, which I discovered when I forgot to throw some away and found that they had dried beautifully!

Stand the flower heads in about 2in (5cm) of water, having first stripped off all the leaves and bashed the ends of the stems. You can dry them in any part of the house, but they will dry quicker if they are in a warm, dark room. Do not leave the flowers in the water once they have dried.

An old fashioned wash bowl and jug containing eucalyptus leaves and mimosa stems, which have been preserved with glycerine and which beautifully complement the colours of the china.

HOW TO STORE YOUR FLOWERS

When your flowers have been dried you will probably find that you will not need to use them all at one time, and frequently a summer display will be put away to be replaced by an autumn one, and so on. Knowing how to store both the flowers you have dried, but not yet used, and completed arrangements is very important, for it would be a great shame to waste all the work you have done during the spring and summer.

An outhouse, a barn, a preserves cupboard or even under the bed are all suitable for storing flowers, but it is essential to find somewhere that is fairly permanent so that you do not have to keep moving them around. Wherever you choose should be dry and cool. Some people prefer to leave the flowers hanging if they have sufficient space in an outhouse, and this is the most economical way if you have the space, particularly for very large quantities. If this is done, the flower heads should be covered with paper bags, which should be carefully secured to prevent the colours fading and dust accumulating on the petals.

If the quantity is reasonably small, a box such as a shoe box, or a larger cardboard box of the kind often obtainable from florists, or a large basket with a lid are best. Punch a few holes in the sides of the boxes to allow ventilation. Wrap the flowers carefully in tissue paper, taking great care not to squash them and placing the paper quite loosely around them. Do not store too many bunches in one box as the weight of the top bunches could damage those below; three layers is enough. Place a piece of tissue paper between each layer. Individual flower heads take up less space, and many can be stored at once. Lay each head in tissue and place a thick piece of tissue between the layers.

Flowers that have been preserved using a desiccant should be stored in a cardboard box with a lid. A thin layer of silica gel should be placed on the bottom of the box and each layer of heads separated by tissue paper.

Never store flowers in plastic bags or plastic containers; the flowers will sweat and then rot.

LEFT: some of the flowers that can be dried successfully. (See pages 40-2.)

OPPOSITE: hydrangeas standing to dry in a little water while some already-dry flowers are being carefully packed before being stored.

PAGES 36-7: a sophisticated display made with lavender, which was cut to even lengths, and a border of peonies, marjoram and pink tulips, which were dried in silica gel.

ARRANGING DRIED FLOWERS

During recent years dried-flower arrangements have become almost as natural a part of interior design as an ornament or a picture. Many stores specialize in the sale of dried flowers, and ready-made arrangements are available in numerous shapes and sizes. It is also possible to find shops that will make to order. The cost of having a display made for you can vary in price, but it is generally quite high and not nearly as rewarding as making your own.

You will most probably already have quite a range of vases, baskets, pots and jugs, most of which can be used for dried-flower arrangements. Study the shapes carefully and then select dried materials with interesting shapes and textures to fill and complement them. Colour is important, and it is wise to consider the colours of the room in which you wish to place the display before rushing out to buy a mass of flowers. For example, you might choose a colour to match the curtain fabric or wallpaper or even some other feature you wish to highlight. Alternatively, choose a contrasting colour, which will make the arrangement a pleasing feature of the room without dominating it.

There are a number of things you can do to ensure success. First, if you have never attempted to make an arrangement, try not to be over-ambitious. Choose a small idea, which will give you an opportunity to acquire some confidence without incurring huge costs. Choose colours and shapes that will look pleasing once they are in position. There are no rules to the type of style you choose, and everyone will create something totally different.

Many types of dried flowers are sold commercially in a wide range of outlets: you can buy from a village fête or from a large store. The variety to choose from can be almost overwhelming, for flowers for drying are grown all over the world and are increasingly available from specialist shops. Some types, such as African seed pods and Australian banksias, are particularly exotic and could be used if you are unable to find your own supply of large cones and seed heads. Specialist shops are also invaluable for providing large amounts of filler flowers, which are so useful for beginning a display, and they can usually be found there in good quantities. Sea lavender is particularly versatile, and commercially grown bunches can be added to your home-grown selection without looking out of place.

Making a display is really not as hard as it may appear. Many people feel nervous about handling dried flowers because they look so fragile. Some types of flowers do, indeed, shed their petals while you are arranging them – this is quite natural – but once the display is finished they should not drop unless disturbed. A gentle squirt of hair-spray will usually solve the problem! Although you can handle some dried flowers such as grasses, sea lavender, amaranthus or flax and other, non-multi-petalled varieties quite normally, flowers such as roses, helichrysums and peonies should be handled gently. These flowers have brittle heads, which will snap off easily. Never attempt to push a flower stem into a display by applying pressure on its head. Many of these types of flower will benefit from being wired before you begin to prepare your display, particularly if it is to be placed where it may be disturbed by heavy household traffic.

 # CONTAINERS

Your choice of container will largely depend on the type of display you wish to make, the size that it is to be and where it will be placed. You should consider this last factor even if the display is to be a gift – it will be all the more appreciated if you have taken it into account. We are often inspired to make a display after purchasing a wonderful vase or basket. Then the decision-making process will operate in reverse, and you will have to decide where the finished arrangement will look best.

Usually you will have a wide choice of containers at home: an old pot or a vase that no longer holds water can be ideal for a dried-flower display, and even a pretty, but cracked vegetable dish, no longer serviceable at table, can make a welcome reappearance.

OPPOSITE: just some of the containers that can be used for dried-flower arrangements.

Your imagination is the key to success. Interesting containers can often be found in junk shops and at jumble sales, village fêtes or antique markets. You might come across almost anything, ranging from wonderful old chamber pots or ancient tin baths to pretty china cups and dishes. Earthenware and terracotta are simply made for rich autumnal displays, selections of grasses or lavender, but even simple garden flowerpots can look specactular. The choice is yours.

If you are attempting your first display, avoid containers that have very narrow necks, as these quickly become hard to arrange. It is also wise not to use wide-brimmed containers for your early attempts as they swallow up huge amounts of flowers. These could be tried when you have gained more experience.

Baskets are perfect for dried flowers, their rather rustic appearance suiting the muted colours of dried materials. Because they are usually rather light in weight, it is advisable to use Drihard clay rather than plastic foam (Oasis) blocks. The clay gives greater stability and helps to prevent your finished arrangement from being easily knocked over. There are numerous wonderful baskets available commercially, which can be purchased from good florists and from specialist stores. Sizes range from tiny, fingertip deep baskets, which are perfect for making place-settings, to enormous, cavernous log baskets, which need huge quantities of flowers but in which you can simply place whole bunches to create a delightful, informal effect. If you are trying to achieve a particular colour scheme, you could try painting the basket with a quick-drying spray paint; this can look stunning, and it is a very useful way of supplementing colour if your flower choice is limited.

There are several ways of adding height to your container. You can fill it with paper or with sand so that you can wedge the plastic foam block near to the brim and so begin your display from the top of the container. Alternatively, extra length can be created by attaching additional wiring to longer-stemmed flowers.

SHAPES

Whichever type of container you have selected, you will probably require a background filler. It is preferable to choose a neutral colour, which will blend with the flower colours you have chosen. Cream or green are ideal, and there is a wide variety of types to choose from. Filler materials have the advantage of using up a substantial amount of space, and they will help you to create the shape you want for your arrangement. Fillers will also support any less robust flowers that will be added afterwards. Helichrysums are the worst culprits for drooping and, if they are not wired they really must have some support for their heads. Sea lavender (limonium) is excellent for this purpose; its sturdy stems are covered with attractive little pink, white or blue flowers, and the stems have naturally pointed tips, so that you can create the shape you wish without too much effort. Sea lavender can often smell rather musty. This is normal because it is a plant of the salt-marshes, but the smell will wear off very quickly once the flowers are exposed to natural air. Grasses make an attractive base, particularly the stems of oats, which add a pretty, bobbing effect and are perfect for creating dainty displays.

Once you have chosen a filler, the next step is to choose the flowers. Whatever types you choose, the secret is to have as many different shapes as possible and to select the correct quantities. An arrangement can be most unattractive if you can still see the plastic foam, clay or wired stalks when it is completed.

If this is your first attempt, try choosing three or four types of flowers to add to your filler. Keep the colours subtle and make sure that they blend well with one another. When you begin arranging, always use only one type at a time, otherwise you are likely to finish with a bitty, unbalanced arrangement. If your arrangement is to be tall, do not feel that you cannot use small plants; these can easily be wired (see pages 46-7).

Dried flowers are not as flexible as fresh flowers, and there are few types that can be made to hang over the edge of the container.

Some of the shapes and textures that can be achieved with dried flowers: (outside, from left to right) *Gypsophila minima*, heather, echinops, red roses, salvia, pink roses, pink helichrysum, cornflowers, silene, white rhodanthe daisies, cream helichrysum, pink larkspur, green amaranthus, maidenhair fern, old English lavender, nigella (love-in-a-mist), oregano, wheat, phalaris (canary grass), barley, maidenhair fern, oats, 'Hidcote' lavender, maidenhair fern, red amaranthus, alchemilla, blue larkspur, cream larkspur, yellow achillea, pink rhodanthe daisies, pink roses, sea holly and pink poker (*Psylliostachys suworowii*); (centre) carmine-pink peony, gypsophila, deep red roses, orange helichrysum, statice (*Limonium latifolium*), yellow roses, pink helichrysum, deep pink peonies, achillea 'The Pearl', blue delphiniums, white immortelles (xeranthemum), dark pink peony, yellow helichrysum, pink roses, limonium 'Caspia', poppy heads, carmine-red peony, gypsophila and *Gypsophila minima*.

Quantities of leaves that have been preserved in glycerine can help to overcome this problem as they are far more supple once treated by this method and can continue to look almost fresh for a long time.

If you have chosen to make a display for a dining-table, keep the arrangement low so that people seated opposite can see one another. Remember that, although the arrangement is the centre-piece, you should leave room for the other things that will go on the table during the course of the meal. If you have a very large table, a long, narrow arrangement, rather like a swag, running down the centre, can be very pretty. A coffee-table display should also be kept low, and the arrangement should not dominate the space required for glasses or cups. Similarly, the height of a sideboard display should be judged according to the size of the furniture, and the position of the nearest picture or ornament. Displays should always be in proportion to their area.

If you have elected to make a display for a hall table or a fireplace, where the arrangement will not be visible from the back, you can create a flat-backed display, which has the advantage of needing less flower material. If the display is to be placed on a central table, however, you will have to make a circular display, which will be attractive from any angle.

Remember, arranging dried flowers is totally different from arranging fresh ones, so let yourself relax and experiment with confidence. This is not an examination you are about to take, but a pleasurable challenge in creating a display of your own choice.

SEASONAL ARRANGEMENTS

A fresh-looking springtime display made with wheat, oats, delphiniums, love-in-a-mist, cream peonies and salvia. This type of shape is ideal for a low table or for a shelf.

Each of us will conjure up different colour images for the seasons of the year and will be inspired to make arrangements to match them. Your choice may be partly limited by the colour schemes within your home, but it is usually possible to find at least a couple of areas that are fairly neutral – a plain-coloured wall, for example, or some wood panelling in the kitchen or perhaps a fireplace with a brick surround.

Spring colours might reflect the first woodland flowers: the yellows of Easter or the new, lush green foliage that is rapidly appearing on plants and trees. Late spring and early summer sometimes seem to run into each other, inspiring us to make arrangements from warmer, peachy-coloured materials to match the improving weather. By the time summer arrives we are often overcome by the stunnng array of garden hues and the abundance of brilliantly coloured

soft fruits – strawberries, raspberries and blackcurrants. With so many colours available to us, it is easy to let our imaginatons take over. You will generally have to wait until your harvested fresh flowers are dry before you can begin to make displays with these wonderful colours, but you can usually use flowers from the previous year if you have stored them carefully. Peonies appear early in summer and take little time to dry. They are one of the rare, large-headed flowers that can be dried successfully and, since they last such a short time while fresh, I never feel guilty about gathering as many as I can from the garden, so that I can dry and enjoy them for the rest of the year!

Autumn is the one season that inevitably dictates its colours to us. The changing leaves, the nuts, the cones and the berries are rich in rusts, deep reds, oranges and browns. Many beautiful displays can be

A bowl of dried *Helipterum roseum* (acroclinium) daisies ornament a breakfast table.

OVERLEAF: a traditional Welsh dresser filled with sparkling china and decorated with a small oblong vase containing a mass of roses with a border of gypsophila.

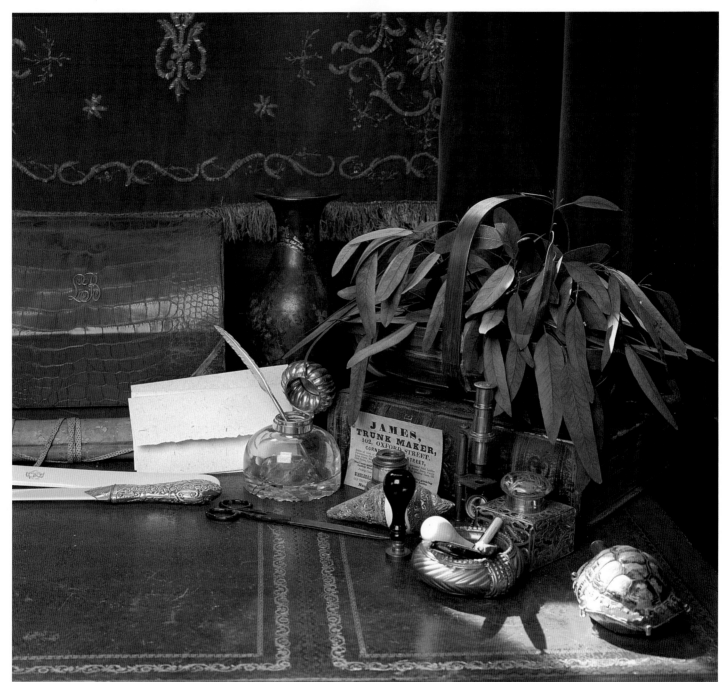

made at this time, and you will be able to add many of your dried summer flowers to elegant stems of beech and clusters of plump cones.

In winter we will want to make colourful displays to cheer up the grey days or arrangements in shades of blue to represent the cold outside. Christmas, the biggest celebration of all, can be a riot of colour;

displays can include flowers sprayed gold, silver or bronze as well as the traditional reds, greens and creams. Ribbons can give a special festive touch.

Dried flowers adapt beautifully to any season, and their muted colours often reflect our moods. As with any type of attractive ornament, a stunning seasonal display will enhance any interior.

A simple display that would be ideal for a gentleman's study. The trug is filled with eucalyptus stems, which have been preserved using glycerine.

WIRING DRIED FLOWERS

When you have selected the flowers you want to arrange, you will probably find that some of them need wiring. It could be that an individual flower head needs a wire, or that a cluster of flowers would look better wired together to create volume, or that an existing stem has to be attached to a longer wire so that it can be placed in a large arrangement. There is a special technique for each of these.

WIRING A FLOWER HEAD

Take the head between your fingers and insert the wire under the flower, pushing it through slightly to one side of the head. It is unwise to try to push the wire straight

through the centre of the flower, as this will usually cause it to disintegrate.

As you begin to push the wire through, gently place your thumb on the centre part of the flower, where you feel the wire will appear. It is important to push down with your thumb to exert just enough pressure to prevent the wire suddenly breaking through and so damaging the head. When wiring roses, peonies or similarly shaped florets, hold the head firmly between your fingers, pinching in gently to support the flower. As

RIGHT: wiring a peony head and (above right) binding the wire to a longer piece.

Wiring a cluster of flowers together so that they can be included in a display or added to a garland, swag or bouquet.

the wire begins to break through, push down gently to prevent the wire from shooting up, which could ruin the flower head.

With any type of flower head, once the wire appears, pull it through high enough to make a small loop (see opposite left), which you will then pull down into the flower. The loop prevents the wire from slipping out. While you are pulling the loop down, follow it in with your finger to make sure that it does not go too far; it should sit tightly in the base of the flower head. Once the head has been wired, you can, if you wish, secure it to a longer wire, ready for insertion into the arrangement (see opposite right).

WIRING CLUSTERS OF FLOWERS TOGETHER

Small bunches or clusters of flowers can be wired together to create volume for your display, and bunches like this are especially useful if you are making a very large arrangement or if you are repeating a particular design around the edge of a bowl or basket. If large flower heads are in short supply, you could wire together a group of small flowers – a mass of achillea 'The Pearl', which will form a fluffy cream pompon, for instance, or a cluster of brightly coloured statice – to replace larger heads such as hydrangeas or peonies.

To create this effect, collect all the heads together, keeping the flowers level with each other, then secure them by binding firmly under the heads. Continue to wind the wire right down the stalks until they form just one stem, which can be inserted into the display. When you are wiring mixed flowers, arrange the different heads at the heights you want, then start to secure them several inches (5-6cm) down the stems away from the heads. Continue wiring down the stems to make it easier to place the group in the display. Judge the final stem length you require, and cut the wire accordingly.

MAKING A DISPLAY

The accessories you will need to make an arrangement: (back, from left to right) reels of paper ribbon, containers, Oasis (plastic foam) shapes and baskets; (centre, from left to right) baskets, reels of ribbon, wires and cutting equipment in a jar and a selection of containers including a teapot; (front, from left to right) a selection of dried flowers, a partly made arrangement in a basket, a reel of wire, tape for the plastic foam, a craft knife, flower clips (in a small basket), Drihard clay, glue and dried flax.

YOU WILL NEED

A clear, flat surface

An old cloth or sheet (optional but advisable)

Flowers

A container

A plastic foam (Oasis) shape or Drihard clay

Plastic flower clips

A reel of wire

A selection of stubb wires

Glue

Strong scissors

Accessories such as ribbons

AN ALL-ROUND DISPLAY IN A POT OR BASKET

When you are arranging dried flowers the most important factor is to have plenty of space. A large kitchen table or work-top area on which you can spread out all your ingredients is essential. It is also useful to have several fairly large empty jars or baskets to hold materials that you will not be using immediately. If you have too many types on your working surface at one time, they will become muddled and tangled.

The first step is to stick the flower clip into your container. If you are planning to make several arrangements, it is best to complete the gluing of all the clips at this stage, since the glue can take up to 30 minutes to dry. Take the plastic foam or clay and press it

The three main stages in making an all-round arrangement.

This brilliant blue vase is filled with cornflowers, oregano, salvia, marjoram and trachelium (throatwort). The large, pastel-coloured basket standing on the floor contains a selection of flowers – larkspur, gypsophila, statice, roses, rhodanthe daisies, pink poker and silene.

A table display and matching place-settings. This summery basket has been made so that it looks attractive from every angle (see All-round Displays on page 48). The basket and the dill have been sprayed white, and the other flowers include eucalyptus stems, bobbles of brunia and delicately shaded, peach-coloured roses, which have been preserved in silica gel. The place-settings were made from little clusters of dill, eucalyptus and a single rose, tied together with narrow satin ribbon.

down on to the clip, securing the base firmly to the bottom of the container. If you have chosen to use clay, it is important to place enough on the clip to support at least 2-3in (5-8cm) of the stalks. If you are using heavier stems, such as beech, you will find that they will start to slip if they are not well supported by the base.

Dried flowers do make the most dreadful mess, and it is a particularly good idea to place a cloth under the flowers to catch any shed petals or leaves. This is vital if you are working in a carpeted area! The cloth can be folded inwards at the end of your work and emptied outside. If you are fortunate enough to have an outside workroom with a wooden or linoleum floor, the mess can easily be swept away.

The best way to begin working is to take each bunch of flowers in turn and to prepare the lengths you require for your display, wiring any frail heads that are not sufficiently strong for arranging. You may find that you will need to wire more flowers during the course of the arrangement if you find you want extra style or height. To judge the lengths for your container, hold the bunches against the side to give you an idea of the height you want from the brim. Do not cut all the lengths at once; you may find you want some taller flowers from the bunch later on.

The first material to be placed in the container is the filler. As this is how the shape will be formed, it is important to take time over this stage. Place the stems of the filler material around the edge of the container to give an even, all-round effect and check that the lengths are more or less equal so that the display will look attractive from any angle. The filler should normally protrude 1-3in (3-5cm) from the edge (see left-hand illustration, page 49). Keep turning the container to obtain an even balance to the display. The next step is to establish the central height. Place a piece of the filler in the centre of the base material so that you can judge this, then place three or four slightly shorter pieces just below the central piece. Continue working in this way, slightly shortening the pieces for each row as you work down to meet the edge filler (see centre illustration, page 49).

When you are attempting your first displays you will probably find that you make the arrangements too flat, rather like cushions. You can help to avoid this by angling the stems and not placing them in the basket as if they were flattened grass! Make sure that the central pieces are put in as straight as possible to create a spiky effect. Another mistake is to keep the stems too long so that you end up with a huge display with unsightly gaps to fill. All these are

The three stages in making a flat-backed arrangement for a vase.

An antique brass container looks splendid filled with maidenhair fern and with roses and peonies, both of which were preserved in silica gel.

common errors, so don't be afraid to experiment or to be critical – you will quickly find the best ways of working.

When you are happy with the overall shape and proportions of the filler, you can begin to place the flowers into the display. Always use all of one type before going on to the next. If you have a pointed variety, such as larkspur, use these first to create the colour shape. Distribute the stems evenly around the display, making sure that there are no great blocks of colour in any one place. As with the filler stage, keep turning the display until you are satisfied with the result. Continue to work through each bunch until you have finished the arrangement (see right-hand illustration, page 49).

ARRANGING A DISPLAY IN A VASE

When you are arranging flowers in a vase much of the shape will be determined by whether the display will stand in the centre of a surface, against a wall or in a fireplace. (Such considerations could, naturally, also apply to a basket.) If the display is to be central the arrangement must be done in the round, as with the all-round display described above, but, when you are using a vase it is not always best to place the filler in first. It is often better to arrange any spiky stems that will help you obtain the height and shape you want first of all, then add the filler, then the selected flowers (see illustrations, page 51).

If the arrangement is to stand against a wall or is to be placed in a firelace you could make the display flat backed. This method is ideal if the arrangement is not going to be moved around, and it will economize on materials. A flat-backed display will be viewed from the front and sides, so it is important to arrange the flowers at the level from which they will be seen: if the display is to stand on the hearth, make the arrangement on the floor to ensure that it will be attractive when seen from above.

A DISPLAY USING ONE TYPE OF PLANT MATERIAL

A display made from only one type of material can look very stylish and would be ideal for a reception room.

You should try to obtain a square or rectangular container, 4-6in (10-15cm) deep.

Place two flower clips at equal distances from each other and from the ends of the container, and then completely fill the space with a plastic foam block, which should touch all the sides. If you find that one block is not large enough, but two are too big, cut the second one into pieces to fill the gaps.

The best plants for this kind of display are tall, straight-stemmed types, such as lark-

A display made entirely from even lengths of wheat tied with a large paper bow.

spur, delphinium, wheat, lavender and some varieties of rose. All the stems should be kept as long as possible and cut so that each stem is the same length. Excess leaves should be removed at this stage, except on the roses, the leaves of which can look attractive, although they are sometimes too brittle to survive the process of arranging and disintegrate as you work.

Start by placing a row of stems down the centre of the container and then work along each side in turn until you reach the outer edges. Keep the stems as close together as you can. When you have finished, you can either tie the stems with a bow or fill the edges with shorter flowers such as roses, hydrangeas, peonies or gypsophila to form a stunning border.

USING DRIED FLOWERS

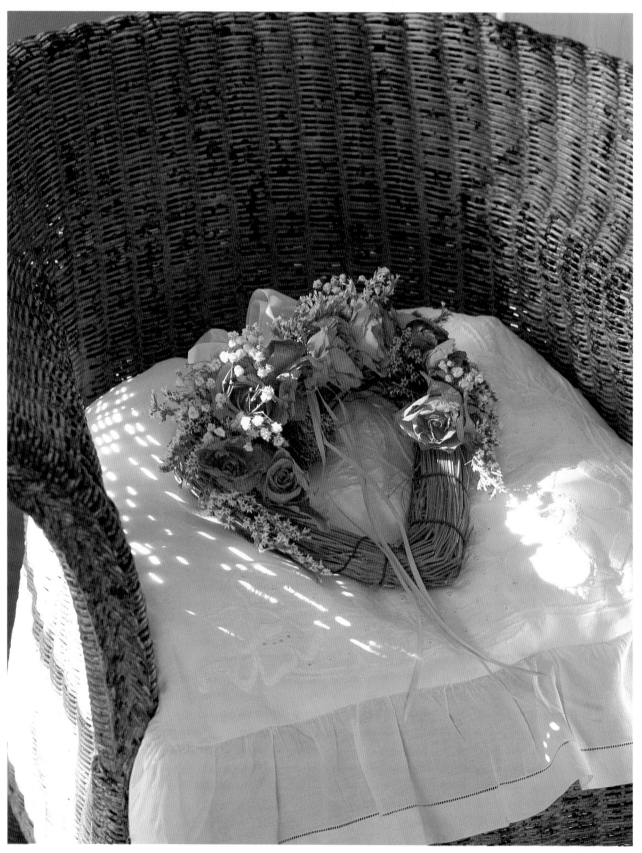

A VALENTINE HEART

Valentine's Day is the first festive occasion of the year and, according to some legends, the day of the rose, when, traditionally, flowers and cards are sent anonymously to surprise the receiver. It can be as much fun to send a gift to someone as to receive one, and instead of sending fresh flowers, which will last such a brief moment, you might prefer to send a gift made of dried flowers, which will last for months. This Valentine heart is very romantic; it is also simple to make and requires few ingredients.

YOU WILL NEED

A heart-shaped frame (the one shown is made with lavender)

Thin stubb wires

Strong glue

10-12 dried roses (preferably dried in a desiccant)

Small quantity of sea lavender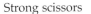

Small quantity of gypsophila

Strong scissors

Wire cutters

Pink or matching ribbons to decorate – 12in (30cm) of medium width satin ribbon and 24in (60cm) of narrow satin ribbon

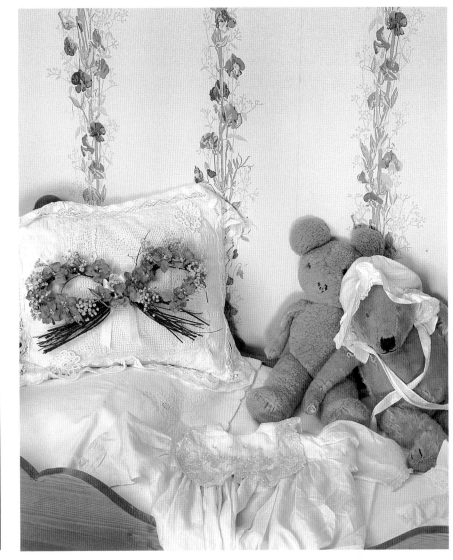

This heart is decorated in much the same way as a garland (see page 63). Before you begin you may need to place wires through the roses to lengthen their stems.

Take a very small amount of sea lavender, gypsophila and one rose and bind them into a little bunch. Do this ten or twelve times, depending on how many roses you have chosen, then, beginning at the top of the heart, bind the bunch on to the frame using the stubb wires. Complete this as neatly as possible, making sure that the wire ends are finished off and are as invisible as possible. Work to approximately half-way down one side of the heart, then repeat the process on the other side. It is, of course, possible to decorate all the way round if you wish, but the shape of the heart sometimes seems to disappear. If a rose head snaps or a flower is too fragile to wire, make the little bunches of sea lavender and gypsophila only and glue

the roses on afterwards. When you are pleased with the result, make a bow with the medium width satin ribbon and some trailing tails with the narrow ribbon. Place a thin wire through the back loop of the bow, gather the tails as well, and attach it to the top of the heart.

If you are sending it through the post, pack the Valentine heart into a cardboard box filled with plenty of tissue paper.

A DECORATED BOW FOR A NEW BABY

It is sometimes hard to think of original presents for new-born babies, especially if the baby is not the first-born in a family, which will normally already have all the baby clothes it needs. The best type of present will be one that is decorative and lasting, and it will be particularly appreciated if it has been made by you.

A pretty twig bow decorated as a gift for a new-born baby. Blue delphinium flowers and gypsophila have been used, and the decoration is completed by a bow with trailing ribbons.

OPPOSITE: a Valentine heart made with a frame of woven lavender stems decorated with sea lavender, roses preserved in silica gel and gypsophila. A bow and trailing ribbons have been attached to the centre of the heart.

An Easter basket made from daffodils and tulips, which have been preserved in silica gel.

Make tiny bunches of gypsophila and ensure that they lie quite flat on the bow so that there is a central space in which to glue the delphinium heads – blue ones for a boy, pink ones for a girl. Work all around the bow but leave the trailing parts free of decoration. Put a tiny spot of glue on each delphinium head and press the flower firmly between the clumps of gypsophila, leaving equal spaces between each one. When you have completed this stage, tie the ribbon into a bow and attach this to the centre, leaving some tails to trail down beyond the decoration.

This pretty bow could be hung on a wall or placed on the nursery door.

AN EASTER BASKET

Easter is one of the major festivals of the year, and Easter Sunday in particular is a colourful day and one that children adore. I remember that when I was tiny we would hunt in the garden for secret nests, which had apparently been built by rabbits! I can vividly recall finding the nest that was meant for me: it was placed beneath a huge clump of daffodils and contained clusters of tiny eggs, chocolate rabbits and real eggs, beautifully decorated with delicate transfers. I will never forget that moment, and a nest like that is certainly a most delightful way to surprise a child. Each year I follow the daffodil theme and make a basket with preserved daffodils, carefully dried in a desiccant. The flowers retain their colour extremely well and provide an original display for an Easter decoration within your home.

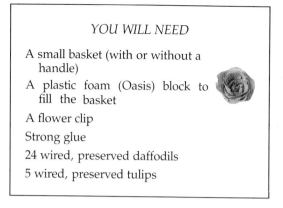

YOU WILL NEED

A small basket (with or without a
  handle)

A plastic foam (Oasis) block to
  fill the basket

A flower clip

Strong glue

24 wired, preserved daffodils

5 wired, preserved tulips

Coat the flower clip with glue and place it in
the base of the basket, pressing it down
firmly, and leave it to dry. Push the Oasis on
to the clip, cutting away any excess. Take
each daffodil in turn and begin the display
by placing those with shorter stems around
the rim. When you have completed the
whole circuit, begin again, placing slightly
longer flowers above the first. Continue in
this way until you reach the centre of the
basket, where the flowers will be higher than
those around the edge (see the photograph
on pages 56-7). When you are satisfied with
the result, place two tulips in each side,
making sure they are evenly spaced, and
one in the centre. The result should be quite
full so that it is not possible to see the plastic
foam beneath. When spring is over you
could wrap the flowers individually in tissue
paper and store them in a cardboard box,
with a small quantity of silica gel powder in
the bottom to keep the box dry.

A CHRISTMAS DISPLAY

Christmas displays are traditionally made
with evergreens, cones and red berries, but I
think it is fun to break with tradition
occasionally and to create a display that will

YOU WILL NEED

A basket

12 fir cones (choose different shapes and sizes)

3 dried peony heads in full bloom

6 hydrangea flowers

3 stems of Chinese lantern pods

Dried grasses

Eucalyptus pods

Adiantum fern

Gold (or silver) spray paint

the floor or over a large work surface. If you have a garden, it would be even better to spray these things outdoors to avoid any mess and to avoid inhaling the spray paint. If you do spray inside, remember to ensure that there is good ventilation from an open window or door.

Place one type of dried material on the paper and spray it as evenly as possible. Leave to dry for a few minutes – it will be

be completely different yet retain the feel of this special day. This basket is made by spraying all the dried-flower material with gold paint.

Take plenty of newspaper and place it on

OPPOSITE AND BELOW: a stunning Christmas display made by spraying all the dried flower material with gold paint. The basket contains a selection of fir cones, peonies, hydrangea flowers, eucalyptus, Chinese lanterns and grasses, arranged around maidenhair fern.

Edwardian-style straw hats are ideal for wearing at summer weddings. The hat on the left has been decorated with yellow roses, lupidium and gypsophila. Matching bows have been placed between the flowers. The hat on the right has been decorated with amaranthus, peonies, statice and larkspur. A large pink bow has been attached to the back of the hat so that the ribbons trail attractively over the brim.

fairly quick if you do not saturate the plants – then turn it over and spray the other side. Do the same to the other plants. When all the plant material has been sprayed and is completely dry, arrange it in the basket, preferably into a base of Drihard clay, which will give weight to the basket and help to prevent the material from becoming top heavy (see page 40). This arrangement could be packed away after Christmas and brought out in subsequent years.

WEDDINGS

Spring and summer are often chosen for weddings, and if you would like to give one of your hats a new lease of life, you could follow true Edwardian tradition by decorating a straw hat. The Edwardians used many different types of flowers, many of which were made from material, packed tightly

round the brim to create a most attractive and very original effect. Dried flowers can look extremely pretty on straw hats, and it is fun to transform completely an old straw hat or even an inexpensive sun-hat.

DECORATING HATS

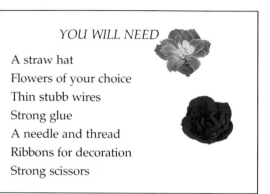

YOU WILL NEED

A straw hat
Flowers of your choice
Thin stubb wires
Strong glue
A needle and thread
Ribbons for decoration
Strong scissors

The first step is to make your choice of flowers into small bunches. Secure these bunches around the brim using thin wires or a needle and thread, whichever you find the easier, and if there is a ribbon around the brim, you will need to sew through both the ribbon and the hat, as the ribbon will become too heavy if it is left unattached. Larger flowers – roses or peonies, for example – look most attractive, and, mixed with the smaller flowers, will fill the brim more economically. If a flower head breaks, glue it on to the bunches. When you have completed the part of the hat you wish to decorate, tie the matching ribbon into a bow and attach it to the back of the hat, leaving some tails to hang down. Alternatively, you could add little bows in with the bunches at even spaces around the brim. Whichever type of bow you choose will look pretty and will give the decoration an attractive finish.

A GIFT FOR THE BRIDE

Making a personal gift for the bride is a wonderful way of showing your friendship. A basket of dried flowers will not only make an attractive, lasting gift but it will be a useful decoration in her new home.

YOU WILL NEED

An attractively shaped basket, tinted in a pastel shade

A mass of gypsophila

Dried rose buds for the rim

A plastic foam (Oasis) block

A flower clip

Strong glue

Strong scissors

A wedding gift for the bride – a pretty pastel-coloured basket filled with a cloud of gypsophila and with a border of little pink roses and rose leaves.

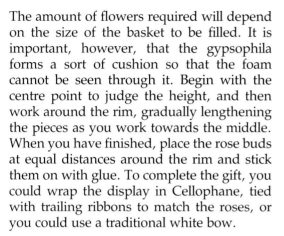

The amount of flowers required will depend on the size of the basket to be filled. It is important, however, that the gypsophila forms a sort of cushion so that the foam cannot be seen through it. Begin with the centre point to judge the height, and then work around the rim, gradually lengthening the pieces as you work towards the middle. When you have finished, place the rose buds at equal distances around the rim and stick them on with glue. To complete the gift, you could wrap the display in Cellophane, tied with trailing ribbons to match the roses, or you could use a traditional white bow.

ACCESSORIES

Wedding accessories made from dried flowers have become increasingly popular because they can be made well in advance and later kept by the bride or her family as a wonderful keepsake. Country weddings are particularly suited to this rather rustic charm, and whole tables can be adorned with swags, little bouquets and baskets. The effect can be delightfully informal and fun to create. Shown opposite are a bouquet and swag made in late summer colours to match the country location. Vivid pink heathers, pink roses, love-in-a-mist pods, pink poker, white larkspur and *Nigella orientalis,* wheat and silene blend beautifully together. The flowers for the swag were made into fairly large bunches and placed on a background of thick plaited rope. The effect is finished with large white satin bows. After the wedding, the swag can be used as house-hold decoration over a fireplace or hung in an archway. The bouquet is made with the same varieties of flowers, alternating and layering each type in turn, and is also finished off with wide satin ribbon, neatly wound around the stems and then made into a large bow (see Swags, page 72, and Bouquets, page 77).

GARLANDS

The art of binding together flowers and leaves to form a ring goes back many centuries. These rings, now called garlands or wreaths, were used by the Greeks and Romans, who made head decorations to mark celebrations or special events. Over the years, garlands or wreaths have never lost their popularity. Nowadays they are most frequently used as pretty head-dresses for weddings, or larger rings are made to adorn our front doors at Christmas-time.

Although they are traditionally made from fresh plants, garlands made from dried materials have recently become popular. The shapes, types and varieties of dried flowers and leaves available commercially offer an enormous choice of rich textures and vibrant colours, and these, combined with any special items of your own, found perhaps in your garden or on a walk, will enable you to create your own personal style.

Dried-flower garlands make beautiful decorations for your home, and they have the great advantage that they are extremely long lasting. A large garland can be hung on a wall in place of a picture, while smaller ones look stunning as table centre-pieces, either on their own or surrounding candle-sticks. These make wonderful decorations, made in delicate shades of pink or blue, are the perfect gift to mark a celebration such as a birth, or a welcoming present for a new home.

One way of making a garland is to bind fresh flowers on to a ring base. If they are left to dry out in a warm, dry place, the shape will form naturally. This method is particularly useful for some types of herb that become rather brittle to work with when dry (see pages 70-2). Herb garlands can be made and hung directly in place, and they do not need to be touched again, unless you rob the ring for your cooking needs! Garlic bulbs, dried chillies and little sweet-corn cobs are attractive additions and create a perfect kitchen decoration. Remember, however, to avoid hanging any sort of dried-flower arrangement near your cooking area or over the sink because the steam will spoil the plants very quickly.

Garlands can be made on a wide choice of bases, depending on the finished effect you want to achieve. Almost any good basket-ware shop will sell a variety of woven wicker, willow or vine rings, while florists usually stock wire and plastic foam rings and probably all the other accessories you will need.

If you wish, you could try making your own base by binding together a mass of straw and using raffia or wire to hold it together. Alternatively, moss can be wired around a simple circle of fairly heavy wire.

Garland bases made from wicker, willow

OPPOSITE: accessories for a country wedding. Both the swag and the bouquet are made with a mixture of heather, white larkspur, pink poker, silene, love-in-a-mist seed pods and a new strain of nigella, *Nigella orientalis,* wheat, white rhodanthe daisies, brilliant pink roses and deep carmine-pink peonies. The arrangements are complemented by wide satin bows.

OVERLEAF: a spring garland: the border is made with myrtle stems, marjoram and preserved daffodils; the garland is made on a wire frame base, packed with oregano and myrtle stems, and the flowers, all of which were preserved in silica gel, include daffodils, tulips, anemones, poppies, alstroemeria, ranunculus and carnations.

or vine are conveniently 'ready made' for poking flowers through the strands, which creates a delightfully informal appearance. If you prefer a thicker effect, you could make up tiny bunches and wire them directly on to the weave, working around to form the circle. These rings look wonderful in a rustic setting, and the bases can be made of either dark, unstripped willow or light, bleached willow. Vine rings tend to be irregular in shape and have a rougher texture.

Wire rings are usually found in two shapes: either completely flat or concave in the centre. I find that the flat rings are easier to use. They have an outer and inner ring, which allow you to build up added thickness and size if you wish. These rings need far more base coverage than the wooden ones, but I think they are more versatile.

Since there is such a wide range of type and colour available, you could try your hand at making a garland to match each season of the year.

SPRING

Spring garlands can be made with the fresh colours of different varieties of daffodils, tulips and anemonies. Although delicate, these flowers are rather fleshy and retain a large amount of water, so it is advisable to use a desiccant such as silica gel to dry them (see pages 30-1). I have had great success with this rather fiddly process, and found my efforts very rewarding. Flowers dried in this way benefit from a very natural backing. Green enhances the flowers, bringing out the very best of their subtle colouring. Moss, oregano, marjoram or ferns are ideal background materials, and the herbs bring added fragrance to the ring. Yellow, which is often associated with spring, particularly Easter, can look wonderful, bringing a welcome splash of colour into the house after a long winter. There are many, many yellow flowers available, including achillea, tansy, lonas, mimosa, helichrysum and some roses, and you may have dried many kinds during the previous summer, carefully storing them until now.

SUMMER

There is such an abundance of choice in this glorious season that by mid-summer, if you are drying your own flowers, you should

have enough material ready for use. The lush and varied textures can make your garland look like an expensive piece of material that blends with your home. Large-headed roses and peonies, dephiniums, achilleas and love-in-a-mist, with a touch of hazy gypsophila, can create the most spectacular garlands, which will remind you of an English cottage garden all through the year.

Subtler shades of pink and peach can conjure up warm, lazy summer days and will blend perfectly with faded chintzes. You might try adding a few fragrant drops of essential oil to your garland to lend extra aroma to the room. Rose or lavender are great favourites and are not too over-powering.

A summer garland: the border is made with gypsophila stems, pink rose heads and little pieces of oregano; the garland is made on a wire frame, packed with hydrangeas and decorated with pink roses, pink peonies and oregano.

An autumn garland: the border is made with little pieces of flax, alchemilla and yellow roses; the frame is packed with beech leaves and decorated with Chinese lanterns, achillea, yellow roses, alchemilla and flax.

OPPOSITE: a winter garland: the border is made with lavender stems and carnation buds; there are pittosporum leaves in the corners, and the frame is packed with tilancia and decorated with pittosporum leaves, lavender and carnation buds.

With so many people getting married during the summer months, a garland makes a perfect wedding gift for the bride, especially if you have made it yourself.

AUTUMN

Autumn is a mellow season of changing colours, as leaves turn wondrous shades of russet, ochre and deep red. It is a time redolent of brisk walks in the country, hot chestnuts and log fires. During early autumn, just before the leaves begin to change, pick some beech, oak and chestnut branches. These leaves, when carefully preserved, will enhance any autumn garland. When you are out walking, hunt for fir cones, nuts, rose-

hips and old man's beard and gather mosses for later use.

Try making a ring using flame-coloured flowers blended with leaves, glycerined until they shine. Alternatively, you could make a base using fir cones and moss, then adding the brilliant pods of Chinese lantern (*Physalis alkekengi*), which grows so rampantly once it is established in the garden. The autumnal colours of these wreaths look lovely in any room of the house, but they are especially attractive when they are hung over a mantelpiece or on a pine door.

Autumn is your last chance to collect vital ingredients for your winter arrangements, as heavy rains will ruin cones and nuts, making them soggy and mouldy. Remember: any material you find should be properly dried before use.

WINTER

Winter can seem so long and drab, but we can wipe out the grey days by adding bright colours to our homes. Blue, which is so often associated with cold, can have quite the opposite effect when it is mixed with brilliant touches of pink or bright red. Blue flowers are usually the hardest to come across, as many blooms are nearer in tone to mauve than to blue. True blues can be found in love-in-a-mist, cornflower, sea holly and some hydrangeas. These flowers always look stunning arranged together, particularly when they are enhanced by a touch of green and cream.

You could mix lavender, larkspur or salvia with little roses or pinks to form a delicately fragranced garland. Try making some garlands for Christmas presents, using some of the flowers you have dried during the summer.

MAKING A GARLAND USING A WIRE RING

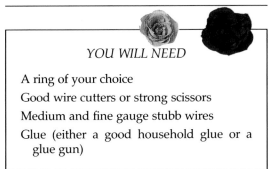

YOU WILL NEED

A ring of your choice

Good wire cutters or strong scissors

Medium and fine gauge stubb wires

Glue (either a good household glue or a glue gun)

First, make up clusters of your chosen base material, making sure that the stems are cut into even lengths. You will need a good quantity of this to give a thick covering. Make as many of these little bunches as you will need in advance so that you do not have to keep stopping. Start by wiring the first cluster on to the ring at an angle (see top illustration). Always work at an angle and keep moving in the same direction. Each cluster must be level on the outer edge of the circle (see centre illustration). If you do not do this, the ring will quickly go out of shape.

When you have completed this process, work out the order in which you will attach the flowers. I find it easier to start with the larger headed types, before filling in with the remaining materials (see illustration at right). Before you attach the flowers to the ring, lay them on top so that you can work out your design and see what it will look like eventually. The ring can be made very simply by using only two or three types of plant material or it can be much more elaborate, with many varieties used. Any delicate flowers that have lost their stems and are too hard to wire can be glued on afterwards. Some people find it easier to glue everything on to the ring. A strong household adhesive will be more than adequate, but make sure that you do not overdo it, since you will clog the petals and the flowers may disintegrate. If you intend making many displays, I suggest you invest in a glue gun, which is quick and by far the easiest way of working without disaster.

THIS PAGE: building up floral material into a garland.

OPPOSITE: getting ready to make a garland: (background, from left to right) hydrangeas, pittosporum, roses and gypsophila; (centre, from left to right) a reel of paper ribbon and an assortment of garland bases; (foreground, left to right) twig bows, a wire ring with several bunches of flowers ready to be attached, reels of wire, scissors and stubb wires.

The wire frame has been packed with bunches of salvia, blue larkspur, bright pink roses and the palest pink peonies. The teapot contains deep pink peonies and salvia.

Give an old mirror a new lease of life by making a garland on a wire frame and by adding three stubb wires, bent to form clips, around the frame to go over the edge of the mirror. The garland contains a base of hydrangeas, echinops, deep red, old fashioned roses and gypsophila.

USING WICKER, WILLOW OR VINE RINGS

Rings made of woody material do not necessarily require a base flower; instead, you could use three or more types of plant material wired together in clusters. After this you can either make a continuous ring or leave little gaps. If you choose to leave little gaps, make sure that you do not leave the joining wires exposed, since they will not only make the ring unattractive but also make it look unfinished. If this is likely to be a problem, you can fill in by wiring or gluing a flower head, cone or bow over the wire.

Rings are not difficult to make into garlands, and, as with all crafts, the more you make, the easier they become. It is a charming art to pass down to our children and a delightful occupation for a rainy afternoon.

MAKING A HERB GARLAND

Dried herbs look extremely attractive hung in bunches and placed *en masse* on a dresser or hung from a kitchen wall, but one of the prettiest ways of displaying them is to place them while they are fresh on a wreath base and to let them dry out naturally in their woven form. Dried herbs tend to be rather brittle and will break and shed easily, and using fresh plants overcomes this problem. You can select any herbs for this project, but preferably choose edible types that can be used in the kitchen and ones that are

YOU WILL NEED

A garland base, on a frame woven from straw, raffia, grasses or moss

Medium gauge stubb wires, 6in (15cm) long

Wire cutters

Strong scissors

3-6 types of fresh herbs

strongly scented such as rosemary, thyme, bay and sweet marjoram.

You will need to be very organized to make this garland and to keep all the different herbs separate. The herbs should have been cut with their stems as long as possible so that they will reach the back of the ring from both the inside and outside edges. Place one stem over the ring to

This garland was made by placing fresh herbs on to a frame made from oats, secured with rings of wire. The herbs, which can be left to dry naturally, include bay, rosemary, chive flowers, thyme, red sage, lemon balm, wormwood and fennel leaves.

Making a herb garland, showing how the plants should be placed on the ring at angles.

determine the exact lengths required. The stems look prettier if they are placed at an angle (see top illustration, page 71), and remember that although the back of the ring will not be visible, it must still be tidy so that it hangs properly. The sides will be visible from different angles, so they must look as attractive as the front. Cut several stubb wires in half and bend each wire in half again to form a loop (see right hand illustration, page 71). These loops will be used to secure the herb stems into the ring.

Take several stems of one type of herb, and fasten them diagonally across the ring. Repeat this process, placing three bunches evenly around the ring (see main illustration, page 71). Then go to the next type of herb, working as closely as possible to the previous type. If you find that the loops are squashing the pretty leaves, ease the leaves out gently, letting them rest over the loops to hide them.

Continue working in this way, using one type of herb at a time until the ring is full.

SWAGS

Making a swag takes time and requires great patience; it is not a project that can be hurried.

The herbs, flowers, grasses and garlic bulbs should be placed on the swag at different angles in their own little individual bunches.

Swags can be made to hang horizontally or vertically, but they can be any length you wish. You can create a swag from a variety of backing cords, which you can often improvise by using materials that you have at home. A piece of rope, raffia plaited together to form a thick backing or even an old dressing-gown cord – you can, in fact, use anything that is fairly pliable and will form the requisite length to work with.

The style of swag can vary too. You can make a very thick one by using large

A vertical swag made with mixed herbs and dried flowers and grasses. The swag was made on a base containing garlic bulbs, and it includes deep red roses, marjoram, oregano, lavender, wheat, poppy heads, oats and phalaris (canary grass).

bunches of flowers massed together as illustrated on page 74, while thinner swags can be made by forming little clusters of flowers together and binding them on to the backing. If you wish to make a vertical swag, the backing cord should preferably be flat backed and fairly sturdy to prevent it swaying once in place. The plaits from ready-made bunches of garlic bulbs are extremely useful and provide a firm base to work from. You can even successfully incorporate garlic bulbs into the swag to make an ideal kitchen decoration as illustrated above and in the detail opposite.

Swags are traditionally used to hang across fireplaces at Christmas-time, and they are usually made of fresh evergreen material with added cones and berries. Dried-flower swags are just as stunning, however. Made in a combination of colours to match your room, they can be left in position all year.

Swags can be hung across the top of a kitchen dresser and over an archway, but possibly the most popular way to use them

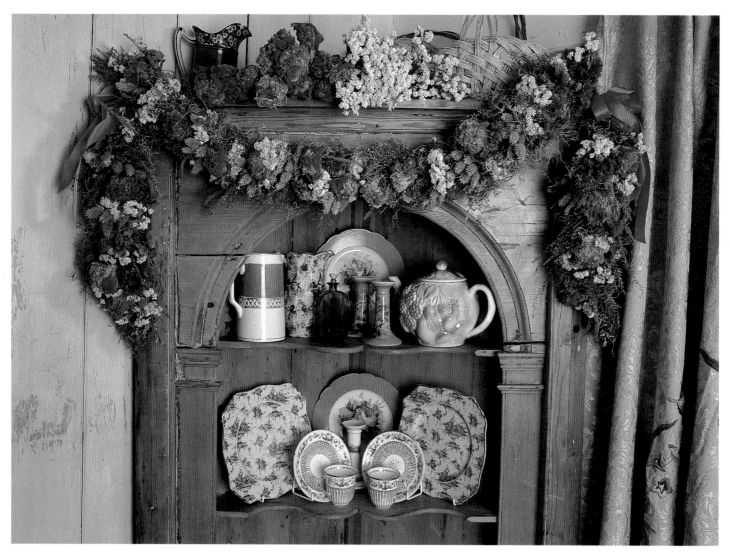

A decorative swag made to run along the rim of the dresser. The swag has been made on plaited rope, and it contains tilancia (moss), peonies, lupidium, blue statice, achillea 'The Pearl', pink poker and phalaris (canary grass). Ribbons complementing the colours of the flowers decorate each side of the swag. On top of the dresser are some peonies and achillea 'The Pearl'.

is at weddings, when they are hung decoratively around the bride's table. Until recently only fresh flowers were used for this occasion, but now dried flowers are greatly favoured as the bride can keep a memento for herself or give the swag as a keepsake to someone dear.

YOU WILL NEED

A length of backing material

Flowers

A reel of thin florist's wire

Strong scissors

Glue (optional)

Accessories such as ribbons

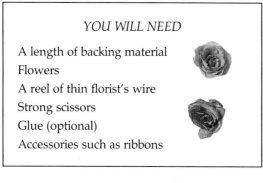

You will need plenty of space to make a swag, and ideally, the backing should be laid out in front of you, horizontally across your working area. The flowers must be cut into the lengths you require and wired into little bunches. Make as many of these as you can, or you will find yourself stopping and starting throughout.

If you are using cord, make a loop at each end so that you can hang it up when you have finished. If the cord is too thick to do this, fasten some strong string or wire to each end before you begin; this will also help you to choose your starting point. Tie the wire from the reel around the cord, just beyond the loop. This reel will not be cut during the binding but will be wound around the stems of each cluster until the other end is reached.

Place the first cluster of flowers across the cord with the stem end towards you. Wind the wire two or three times around the cluster to secure it, then take the next cluster and place it at a slightly different angle, but

Making a swag.

This swag running across the top of the mantelpiece echoes the colours of the nearby decorations. The swag, which was made on a base of plaited rope, contains *Gypsophila minima*, lavender, pale pink peonies, achillea and white rhodanthe daisies.

covering the previous cluster's stems (see illustration above). Continue to work in this way until you reach the other end. Take time to inspect the work, and experiment with the positions of each cluster until you are satisfied that you are obtaining the correct shape.

Smaller swags can be made to hang down each side of the main swag, and this is particularly effective around a fireplace. Tie a bow on each loop to hide the joins (see the photograph above).

OVERLEAF: this garland and bouquet have been placed in a north-facing window to avoid direct sunshine. The garland has been made on a woven vine base, filled with deep carmine-red peonies, peony leaves and gypsophila. The flat-backed bouquet contains roses, peonies, gypsophila, maidenhair fern, blue larkspur and pink rhodanthe daisies, and it is complemented by a natural-coloured hessian bow.

BOUQUETS

Bouquets not only look delightful but are relatively easy to make. Informal arrangements can be made very simply, or the bouquets can be extremely elaborate, containing many beautiful colours and varieties of flowers.

Bouquets and posies make attractive decorations for your home, and they look particularly pretty hung on a wall or used to brighten up a dingy corner. They are an excellent alternative to a display in a traditional container, especially if surface space is limited, and small posies are a pleasing gift to take to your hostess at dinner instead of the traditional bottle of wine!

As with all dried-flower arrangements, you will need plenty of space to create a bouquet. Before you begin, lay out the flowers in their individual bunches, separating the stems, so that they are ready for use.

A TRADITIONAL FLAT-BACKED BOUQUET

YOU WILL NEED

- Flowers, some stems with leaves, some ferns
- Strong scissors
- String
- Elastic bands
- A reel of thin florist's wire
- Ribbons for decoration

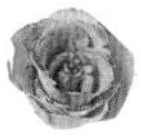

To make a bouquet select flowers that have a variety of shapes and textures and mix these with pretty grasses, ferns and leaf stems. Ferns make the perfect backing, since they are so flat and are not prickly, and the elegant fronds usually have a pointed tip with which you can create the first shape. Flowers that look pretty mixed together in bouquets include roses, peonies, gypsophila, larkspur, achillea 'The Pearl', lavender, daisies and helichrysum. Grasses, particularly oats, wheat, phalaris (canary grass) and barley, are useful for giving movement to the arrangement, while maidenhair fern and bracken fronds are a good choice, and pittosporum and beech leaves add texture.

It is best not to cut any of the stalks until you have finished arranging, since all will be placed into the bouquet at different points, and you could find at the end of your arranging that some do not reach the end if you trim them before you begin.

Take three or more stems of fern and lay them on your working surface in a triangular form, rather like a fan, with the central piece higher than the others to create a pretty pointed shape (see opposite). Then go on to choose the pointed flowers such as larkspur or the grasses, laying them on the ferns at equal distances from each other. Making a bouquet is rather like arranging a vase on a flat surface (see page 52). Keep adding flowers, leaves and ferns until you

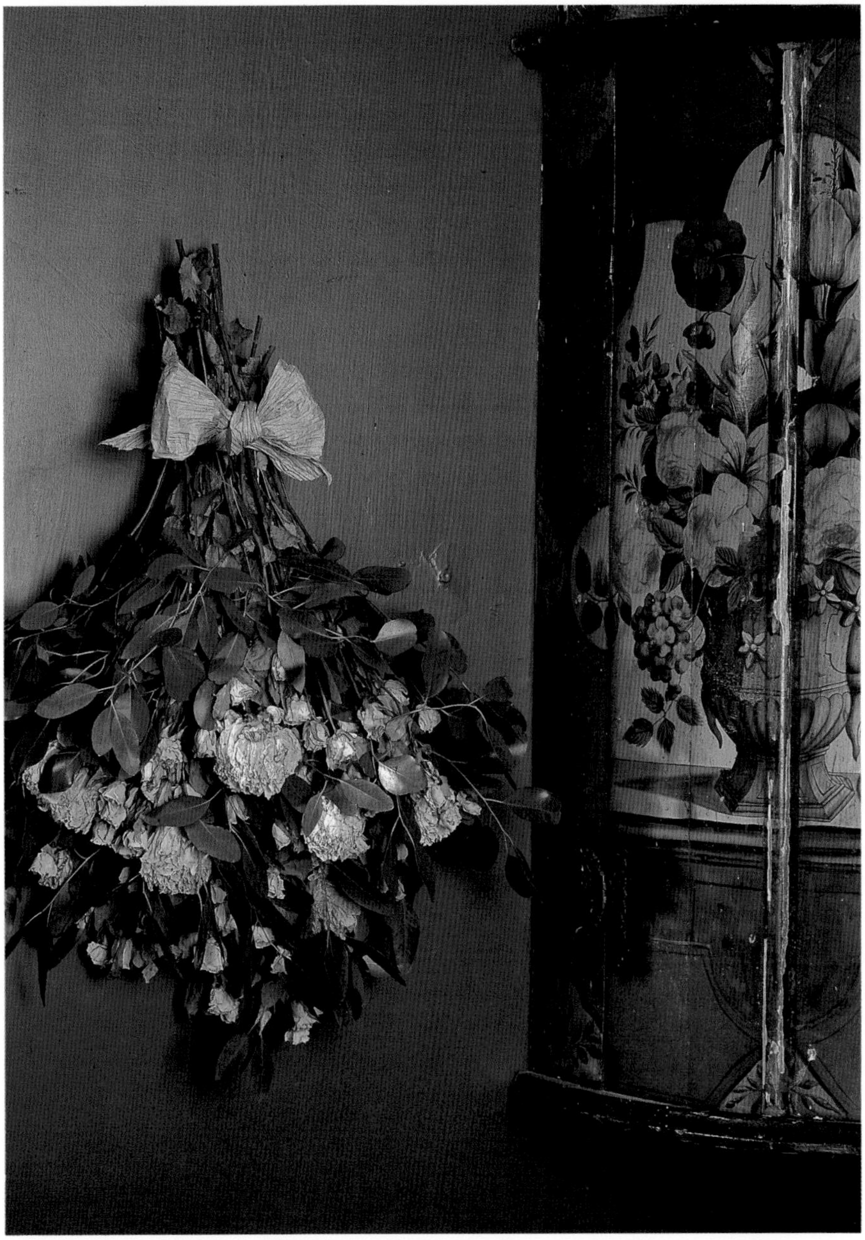

A flat-backed wall bouquet made with eucalyptus leaves, which were preserved using glycerine, pink roses and peonies and then tied with a hessian bow.

Making a tight posy.

have made the bouquet quite plump and high from your surface. Adjust any stems that you think are not placed in properly, then secure them with a piece of string. It may be that some of the shorter stalks, which are not attached to anything, will have to be wired to other stalks within the bouquet, because they will slip down when you have finished all the stem tying. After you have tied the stems with string, wind an elastic band as tightly as possible around the stems above the string (that is, nearer to the flower heads), and then you can snip through the string and remove it. You should use string to secure the stems initially because it is extremely tricky to pick up an unsecured bouquet, and I find that using an elastic band first tends to pull the stems around and so distort the shape of the bouquet.

When you are certain that all the stems are securely held, take a fairly narrow ribbon and wind it around as much of the stems as you wish. Then take some pretty, double-sided satin ribbon and tie an attractive trailing bow.

SMALL POSIES

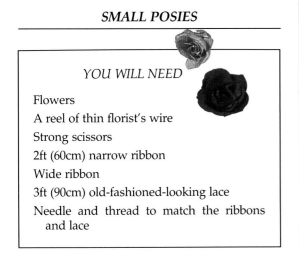

YOU WILL NEED

Flowers

A reel of thin florist's wire

Strong scissors

2ft (60cm) narrow ribbon

Wide ribbon

3ft (90cm) old-fashioned-looking lace

Needle and thread to match the ribbons and lace

Any small-headed flowers are perfect for posies; you could use achillea 'The Pearl', silene, achilleas divided into small pieces, gypsophila, small-headed daisies and little pieces of grasses. Try adding tiny rose buds to complete the effect, and ferns look very pretty in nosegays, or tussie-mussies as they used to be known.

Posies can be rather fiddly to make because you have to hold them in one hand as you work. Begin by forming the flowers into tiny clusters, wiring each cluster carefully. Then take one cluster, which will be the centre-piece, and keep it slightly higher than the remaining clusters, which you place to form a circle around the central one. Keep working in rounds to form a sort of mushroom-shaped mound (see opposite). When you think you have made the shape sufficiently large, secure all the stems as close to the flower heads as possible in order to keep the shape. It may be necessary to wire each circlet as you work, particularly if the flowers begin to slip from your hold.

Take the length of lace and, using the needle and thread, begin to sew around the edge as if you were gathering the lace to form a round skirt (see opposite). Finish off, then take the lace and place it directly

under the flower heads and attach it securely to the stems. I find it useful to give it extra hold by sewing it tightly together and even trying to run one of the stitches through the stems to prevent it slipping down. Then take the narrow ribbon. You will need about one-third of the length to keep as a tail; this will run up the stems under the ribbon you are binding and leave you a tail to tie when you reach the other end. It is best to start at the tip of stems, so adjust the lengths and trim them before you begin. When winding the ribbon round the stems, let each layer lie just over the previous one so that you do not leave any gaps through which the stalks can be seen. Finish off with a knot and then tie the wide ribbon over the knot in a pretty bow (see opposite below).

The tussie-mussie has been made with maidenhair fern, sea lavender, gypsophila and roses, which were preserved in silica gel, and decorated with white satin ribbon. The posy was made by bunching silene together with pink roses, preserved in silica gel. Lace has been gathered around the posy, the stems were bound with satin ribbon and a bow was attached under the lace.

PAGES 80-1: a carpet of bluebells.

Pressed Flowers

For anyone who takes a delight in collecting flowers, pressing is one of the most rewarding ways of preserving them. Unlike bunches of dried flowers, whose life span is limited by wear and tear, sunlight and general household activity, for instance – pressed flowers, once placed in position behind glass or mounted on different objects, have a permanent beauty that will endure for years.

During the last decade, enormous progress has been made in the designs for pressed-flower pictures, and those now sold commercially have both style and imagination, ranging from the simplest flower picture to complicated collages. The wonderful part of pressing, however, is that it is not necessary to press a great quantity of flowers to carry out a project. A small amount of six or eight types will be more than adequate for a beginner and quite sufficient to test your artistic ability.

Collecting flowers for pressing requires both time and care in selecting the most perfect specimens you are able to find. Luckily, it is an inexpensive occupation since many of the flowers, leaves and grasses can be found growing wild or can be picked from your own garden. There are few rules to follow, and experimenting with different varieties to give a range of shapes, colours and textures is part of the fun.

THE PRESSED-FLOWER CALENDAR

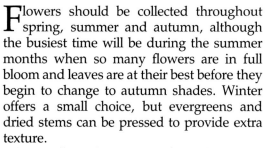

Flowers should be collected throughout spring, summer and autumn, although the busiest time will be during the summer months when so many flowers are in full bloom and leaves are at their best before they begin to change to autumn shades. Winter offers a small choice, but evergreens and dried stems can be pressed to provide extra texture.

You will need to prepare for collecting by obtaining strong scissors, secateurs, masses of blotting-paper and a flower press to take with you for a weekend or a long day trip. These are the minimum requirements; once you have pressed your flowers, you will need other items to complete your projects.

WILD FLOWERS TO PRESS

The guide below lists flowers in the order in which you can begin to search for them, beginning with January, which is still a cold, wintery month, even though the ground may be beginning to warm up in preparation for spring.

Remember to respect nature: resist the temptation to pick every single flower and always leave some flowers behind to produce seed for next year. Although many of the problems associated with flowers becoming extinct are caused by our modern methods of agriculture and by the use of herbicides, over-picking can be just as harmful. Consult the list of protected wild flowers (see page 154) before you set out.

In addition to collecting flowers from the countryside, it is now possible to grow many varieties of wild flower from the seeds that are increasingly available in shops and garden centres. It can be enormously rewarding to devote a patch of your garden to wild flowers, allowing it to become a small meadow, filled with such plants as mallow, field poppies, bellflowers, cornflowers, wild pansies and pink corncockles. By growing your own wild flowers, you will be helping to protect the ever-dwindling varieties that are found in fields and hedgrows, and you will encourage the most wonderful array of bees and butterflies to visit your garden. If you cannot obtain wild flowers from a garden centre, they can also be bought direct from the companies producing them (see page 157).

Opposite: wild flowers and grasses collected for pressing.

Pinks, bluebells, clover, campion and buttercups picked for pressing.

Pussy willow (Salix caprea) February-March. The buds are very tight and grey in February but will be wider in March; press both for different shapes.

Sweet violet (Viola odorata) February-April. Violets will sometimes turn virtually black when pressed. Press the whole stem or the heads alone.

Colt's-foot (Tussilago farfara) March-April. Press the heads, leaves and stems separately.

Lesser celandine (Ranunculus ficaria) March-May. Press the heads and leaves separately or on the stems.

Germander speedwell (Veronica chamaedrys) March-July. Press the whole stem.

Primrose (Primula vulgaris) March-May. Press the flower heads with the stems and press the leaves separately.

Green hellebore (Helleborus viridis) March-May. Press the flowers, stem and leaves together. This plant is poisonous, so wash your hands after touching it.

Wood anemone (Anemone nemorosa) March-May. Press the head, stem and leaves together.

Bluebell (Hyacinthoides non-scriptus) April-May. Although this is rather fleshy, it can be pressed successfully. Press the heads on their own or with the stem cut half-way down, since the base carries too much water. It would be wise to change the blotting-paper after several days, and then again after one week.

Buttercup (Ranunculus acris) April-July. There are different types of buttercup, and some will even be found flowering in September and October if the autumn is warm. Press the whole plant or just the heads. The flowers tend to fade after being exposed to light, so it is permissible to touch up the colour with a little yellow poster paint.

Common dog violet (Viola riviniana) April-June. Press the heads, stems and leaves together or the heads on their own.

Cow parsley (Anthriscus sylvestris) April-June. The most useful flower head, as the exquisite, star-shaped flowers can be used in many different

Daisy (Bellis perennis) January-October. The winter will need to have been fairly warm for you to find this flower in January. Choose a sunny day when the flowers are wide open to pick them, and press the flower heads separately or on the stem.

Hazel or cob-nut (Corylus avellana) January-March. Press the catkins only; the twigs are too hard.

Snowdrop (Galanthus nivalis) January-March. Sometimes snowdrops do not appear until February. They press well, although occasionally turn rather brown.

Grey alder (Alnus incana) February-April. Press the catkins only unless the twigs are very fine.

ways and will dry very white. Dry the stems with the leaves separately.

Cowslip (Primula veris) April-May. Unfortunately this plant gets harder to find each year because of over-picking, which is a great pity, not only for the species but also because it presses so beautifully. Press the whole stem with the flowers; the leaves should be pressed separately.

Fritillary (Fritillaria meleagris) April-May. Press the heads and stems only of this rare plant.

Pasque flower (Pulsatilla vulgaris) April-May. This plant is a relative of the anemone, and its name derives from the fact that it traditionally flowers at Easter. Press the heads on their own with the stalks; any leaves should be pressed separately.

Stitchwort (Stellaria) April-July. There are three species, each of which presses well. Press the whole stem of these plants with the flowers and leaves together.

Sun spurge (Euphorbia helioscopia) April-October. Press the heads on their shooting stems, but first cut off the thick, main stem.

Wild pansy (Viola tricolor) April-September. The flowers press very well. Press the heads on their stems, or the heads on their own.

Common forget-me-not (Myosotis arvensis) April-June. Although widely cultivated, this plant also grows in the wild and is common in woods and hedges. Press the whole stem with the flowers and leaves together. The blue flowers retain their colour extremely well.

Field poppy (Papaver rhoeas) May-August. Although it is very fragile once pressed, this is an extremely pretty flower for decorating lampshades. Press the flower on the stem, or remove the petals and press them individually.

Vetch (Vicia) May-August. There are several different types of vetch, all of which press well, although the flowers tend to darken. Press the whole stem with the flowers and leaves together.

Ox-eye daisy (Leucanthemum vulgare) May-August. Pressing this plant is very much a matter of trial and error – sometimes the heads press beautifully, sometimes the petals will shrivel. I believe that tight pressing is the secret of success.

Red campion (Silene dioica) May-July. The flowers sometimes lose colour when pressed and turn a sort of pale brown; they can, however, retain their colour. I find it is really a question of luck!

Ragged-robin (Lychnis flos-cuculi) May-June. Press the whole stem with the flowers and leaves together. Although the flowers may lose colour, the shape is very pretty.

Red clover (Trifolium pratense) May-September. The flowers can be found during most of the summer. The plump heads need to be pressed hard, keeping the stems and the leaves with the flowers.

Water forget-me-not (Myosotis scorpioides) May-September. Press the whole stem with the flowers and leaves together.

Yellow flag (Iris pseudacorus) May-June. This iris, which is found by water, is very fragile when pressed and becomes translucent. It is wonderful for decorating lampshades.

Common mallow (Malva sylvestris) June-September. Press the head on its own, or the whole stem together with the flower and the leaves.

Dog rose (Rosa canina) June-September. This plant is common in hedgerows. Press the flower heads separately from the stem and leaves. Although they sometimes turn cream or brown, the flowers are beautiful for autumn pictures.

Everlasting pea (Lathyrus latifolius) June-August. The bright pink flowers turn a shade of blue when pressed, and they should be well weighted to ensure good results.

Field scabious (Knautia arvensis) June-September. Press the stems with the heads; press the leaves separately.

Foxglove (Digitalis purpurea) June-September. Press each floret separately. This plant is poisonous, so wash your hands carefully after handling it.

Hare's-foot clover (Trifolium arvense) June-September. Press the plant whole, with the flower, stem and leaves together.

Sweet briar rose (Rosa rubiginosa) June-July. Press the heads separately from the stems and leaves. The pink sometimes survives pressing very successfully.

Toadflax (Linaria) June-October. There are two species of toadflax that will press well, one, *L. repens*, is purple, the other, *L. vulgaris*, is yellow. Purple toadflax should be pressed whole on the

stem with its leaves; the yellow species can also be pressed whole, or the flowers taken off the plant and pressed on their own. This is a useful plant.

Chicory (Cichorium intybus) July-August. Remove the blue flowers from the stems and press them on their own.

Creeping bellflower (Campanula rapunculoides) July-September. Press the flowers, stems and leaves together.

Burnet-saxifrage (Pimpinella saxifraga) July-August. Press the heads individually, or the whole stem together.

Fool's parsley (Aethusa cynapium) July-August. Press the heads individually, or the whole stem together.

Harebell (Campanula rotundifolia) July-September. Press the heads together with the stem.

Heather (Caluna vulgaris) July-September. Press the whole stem with the flowers and leaves together. The plant presses beautifully.

Hop (Humulus lupulus) July-August. Press whole stems, or the flowers separately from the stems.

Meadowsweet (Filipendula ulmaria) June-August. This plant presses beautifully; press the blooms with the stems and leaves.

Nettle-leaved bellflower (Campanula trachelium) July-September. Press the flowers with the stems, or remove flowers and press them separately.

There are many, many other flowers you can try pressing and this list is certainly not definitive, although these are all plants that I have tried and pressed with success. Apart from the flowers, many leaves can be collected during the year, but I usually wait until late summer when I have just about finished with the flowers. Among the leaves

Herb flowers: red stonecrop, marigold, bronze fennel, elecampane (elfwort), marigold, penny royal, pinks, mallow, meadowsweet, gay feather (liatris), green fennel, fennel, salad burnet, curry plant, chives, marjoram, yarrow, nasturtium, cotton lavender, borage and lavender.

OPPOSITE: a garden of pressed herbs.

Herb foliage: ground elder, tansy, yarrow, comfrey, catmint, peppermint, sage, eau-de-Cologne mint, lemon balm, wormwood, applemint, tarragon, salad burnet, wild strawberry and marjoram.

I collect are those of: alder, aspen, beech, black poplar, bramble, common lime, copper beech, English elm, English oak, grey poplar, hazel, ivy, London plane, mimosa, rose, sycamore and weeping willow.

Leaves can be pressed throughout spring and summer and then when they change colour in autumn.

GARDEN FLOWERS TO PRESS

You will probably already have realized that flowers that are bulky are best pressed separately from their stems and leaves. This is because it takes several days to flatten a large flower under weights to the depth of the stem, and meanwhile the stem and leaves will have shrivelled.

Many of the garden flowers listed in Growing Flowers for Drying (pages 11-21) will be suitable for pressing, but here are some common garden plants that you can press successfully: anemone, aubrietia, bells of Ireland (molucella), Californian poppy (*Eschscholzia californica*), campanula, clematis, cornflower, cosmea (cosmos), daffodil, delphinium and larkspur, gentian, geranium, gilia, golden rod, hellebore, hollyhock, iris, lily-of-the-valley, lobelia, love-in-a-mist, malope, pansy, petunia, pinks, rattlesnake weed (polygala), small single roses and larger, double roses (press the petals individually), scabious and tulip (the petals are best pressed individually).

HERBS TO PRESS

Surprisingly, most herbs press extremely well, retaining their colour and shape so well that they are still instantly recognizable. Herbs can usually be pressed whole – that is, with the complete stem and flowers – but the one exception is the marigold. Remove the heads from the stems and press them together but keeping good space between each one. The flower heads retain their stunning orange, although sometimes the petals shed after pressing and have to be glued on individually. If you are not familiar with herbs, label each sheet of blotting-paper before placing it in the press.

Listed below are some herbs that will press successfully: angelica, artemisia, bay, borage, chives, comfrey, cotton lavender, fennel, great burnet, ground elder, herb bennet, lemon balm, lovage, marigold, marjoram, mint, nasturtium, red orach, rosemary, sage, salad burnet, sweet cicely, sweet woodruff, tarragon, thyme, wormwood and yarrow.

Pressed herbs make the most delightful kitchen pictures, bookmarks or finger-plates. And not only are they attractive, but they are a useful indentification guide.

Fresh herbs growing in an herbaceous border.

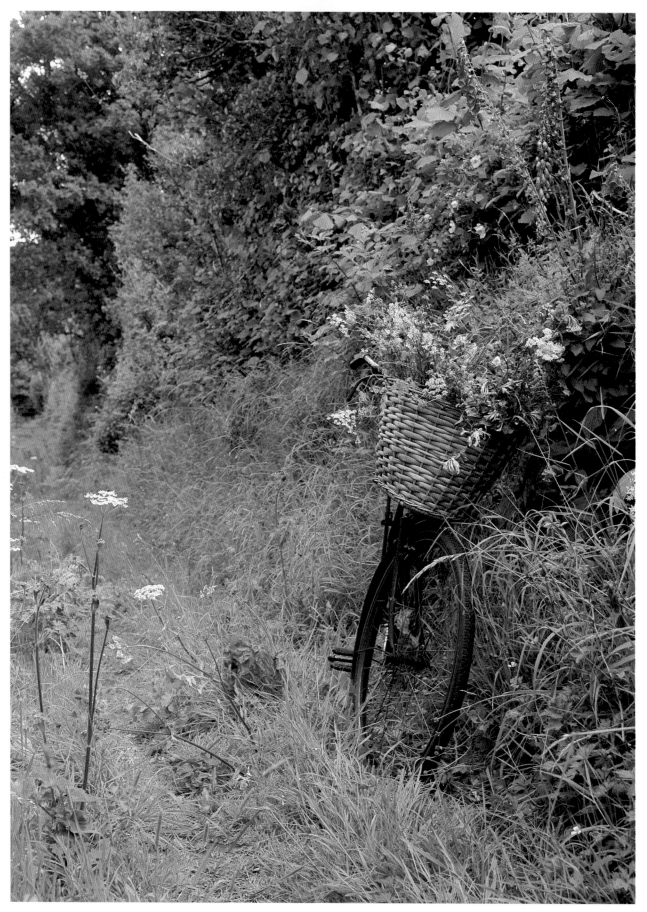

How to Collect Flowers

Many of the same rules apply to pressing plant material as to drying bunches for displays.

The most important rule is to choose only flowers, leaves, grasses and any fresh material that are completely free from rain or dew. The quality of the plant should be the best you can find; make sure there are no browning edges to the petals or the leaves, nor any tears or holes. The plant should be as perfect as possible. Remember that if you press a flower that is not in good condition, the resulting pressed flower will be exactly the same.

Next, you must remember to be well organized for your picking expeditions. You may be in the country, from anything from a few hours to a whole day, and the material you pick must be protected from wilting. It is vital to take some water and jam jars with you, as well as a quantity of absorbent paper. Wild flowers generally wilt more rapidly than the cultivated types, and it is important to get them home quickly in an acceptable condition for pressing.

Try not to pick an unreasonable quantity at one time. You will find it very hard to prepare all the flowers on the same day, and they will not look their best after pressing if you have to leave some until the next day. It is best to decide on the flowers you are going to search for, making a list of, say, six varieties, and to resist the temptation to pick dozens of others!

THE COUNTRYSIDE

When I embark on a trip into the countryside, I find it extremely useful to have a handbook of wild flowers and leaves with me to help identify them and to point out the varieties that are protected (see also page 154). It is also useful to have a small notebook and pencil to list and date your finds.

YOU WILL NEED

Gardening gloves

Secateurs (clippers) or tough kitchen scissors

Jam jars, deep and shallow

Water in a container

Absorbent paper

A flat basket or trug

Elastic bands or string

A deep-sided cardboard box

A large plastic bag

These items are for excursions using a car, and you should create a space to accommodate your cardboard box so that it does not slide about once the vehicle is in motion. I nearly always forget to take a pair of gloves with me and regret that I did for the next three days! Many of the flowers you find will be in the most inaccessible places, often among stinging nettles and in prickly hedgerows. Flowers such as wild roses and honeysuckle always seem to be surrounded by such plants, and your hands and wrists will be scratched if they are not protected. It is also advisable to wear trousers and some thick socks and sturdy shoes!

Wedge the jam jars firmly into the cardboard box, and only when you have begun to accumulate a number of flowers should you fill the jars with about an inch (2-3cm) of water – any more than that could make the stems too wet for pressing and the water might begin to splash out when the car is in motion. Spread the plastic bag over the base of the box to prevent any leaks. The box will help to support taller plant material.

Some plants can be easily picked by hand, but others require secateurs or strong scissors. Try to keep the stems as long as possible, and remember to keep the same varieties

OPPOSITE: collecting herbs in the countryside.

together in bunches when placing them in your basket – it will make sorting far simpler once you get home – and place the bunches in different jam jars. Try to keep at least one window open while the car is not in motion.

Before returning home you may think it necessary to remove all the flowers from the jars. Tip the water on to the absorbent paper and wrap the paper around the base of the stems. Use the plastic bag to protect the bottom of the basket before placing the damp stems in it, and try to keep the bunches a little apart from each other so they do not become tangled.

Leaves collected from trees do not wilt so fast, so, unless you plan spending more than a couple of hours away from home, it will not be necessary to place them in water.

Once home, gently remove the bunches from the basket or trug and remove the absorbent paper. Refill the jars with an inch of water and return the bunches to them to prevent them from wilting while you prepare for pressing.

If your expedition is shorter and on foot, you will only need to take a good shopping basket with a couple of sealed jam jars filled with an inch of water and wedged into the base, plus some absorbent paper, secateurs and gloves. If you are cycling, the same items will be sufficient. A deep cycle basket is important, and I would take a cloth and some pegs for covering the basket before returning home, or you may find there is not much left to press!

THE GARDEN

Selecting flowers and other plant material from the garden is obviously far easier, since you can pick to take account of the quantity of different blooms at different times. This leaves you with plenty of time to organize space to house them all. When you select plant material, choose as many varying colours, shapes and textures as possible to give you far wider choice when the time comes to begin on a project. Picking the same type of flower at different stages will give a more natural feel to a picture; flowers are never all in full bloom at once, and your project will look more real if it includes buds as well as fully open blooms.

Positioning delphinium heads for pressing.

PRESSING FLOWERS

Flowers sometimes take on a completely different appearance when they have been pressed; some varieties change colour completely, while others deepen in tone. Markings that were not very apparent when the flower was picked will heighten with pressing and can become very striking. Leaves normally have a darker and a lighter side, and each can be used, and some leaves can even be persuaded to be twisted while in the press so that both sides can be seen at once. This is particularly attractive when silvery-grey leaves such as those from the white poplar and silverweed are pressed.

Collect leaves throughout the summer to obtain different shades to reflect the way that they change naturally during the seasons. Autumn leaves press beautifully and will dry out very quickly as most of the moisture should already be absent.

As well as pressing individual flower heads, it is also useful to press the whole stem with the leaves and flower together, as long as they are all of a similar thickness. These whole stems are indispensable in giving shape to a pressed-flower design. Some of the large, multi-petalled flowers – roses, for example – should be dismantled before pressing, and each individual petal should be placed on its own. The flower can be re-assembled when it has dried, or you can use the petals to create different shapes or borders.

There are no set rules about which type of flower to press. Although it is often said that certain types simply will not work, I regard that as a challenge, and have had great success with the hardest of all – the iris, the poppy and the petunia. These petals become almost transparent when pressed, and great care is required when removing them from the blotting-paper. If they, or indeed any type, prove stubborn, try running your finger behind the paper, directly under the flower, and the pressure usually bends the paper slightly enabling you to lift the flower off naturally.

OPPOSITE: pressed flowers: cherry blossom, daisies, light blue delphinium, dark blue delphinium, fuchsia, blue hydrangea, pink larkspur, pansies, violas, light red potentilla, rose 'Yesterday', lobelia, cow parsley, light blue larkspur, cosmos, ballerinas, snowdrop, freesia, rose 'Red Robin', purple larkspur, pink roses, anemone, rose 'Ballerina', rose 'Eye Paint', aubrietia, stitchwort, buttercup, small yellow pansies, achimenes, toadflax, white violet, kerria 'Pleniflora', veronica, campanula and melilot.

HOW TO PRESS

There are two main ways of pressing plant material successfully. You can either use a flower press or you can press between strong pieces of blotting-paper.

A flower press is a most useful item to take away with you on holiday or on a weekend trip. It is made from two flat pieces of wood, held together by four long screws and wing nuts, one in each corner. Between these two pieces of wood are layers of blotting-paper and stiff card, which fit snugly within the press and the confines of the screws. The layers begin with a piece of stiff card or board on the bottom of the press, then several layers of blotting-paper are followed by the next piece of card, and so on until it is full. You must begin at the bottom and work your way up, filling each layer in turn. It is not necessary to fill the whole press at once, as you can place extra flowers in at any time you choose. Tighten the wing nuts, which are placed on the screws on the top piece of wood, to secure the press, then tighten them as far as they will go to hold the flowers firmly between the two pieces of wood. Presses are perfect for pressing small blooms and small quantities of flowers. If you are going to press a great amount of material, you will need several presses, and you may even want to make a press using larger pieces of wood to house bigger plant material. Commercially sold flower presses normally come supplied with corrugated cardboard as dividers. I have found that, unless the cardboard is well padded, the ridges often indent themselves on to the plant material, so I would advise you to use strong, unridged cardboard instead.

Select the strongest quality blotting-paper possible, as constant use will quickly wear it out. The blotting-paper should be cut so that it is slightly smaller than the cardboard so stalk ends do not protrude and the card will tighten over the blotting-paper rather than making it curl up around it. **Label each piece of blotting-paper with the type of plant material**. You will go completely mad if you do not do this since more often than not you will fail to recognize the contents once they are pressed, and you will have to open each

piece of blotting-paper to find what you are looking for. It is also wise to keep a record of your pressed materials in a small notebook, marking the date of pressing as well as the variety.

The other method of pressing requires sheets of blotting-paper folded in half and some heavy weights to place on top of them. Large books, a flat cast-iron doorstop or some bricks placed in a plastic bag all work efficiently. When you have put the flowers beneath the folded blotting-paper, place a magazine between each piece to prevent the contents pressing into the one next to it. Place the pieces of blotting-paper on a flat, dry surface, preferably a shelf where they can remain undisturbed. Flowers can take anything up to six weeks to dry completely, although very small or thin, fragile flowers will not take so long. If you require something urgently, you could try placing the material between blotting-paper and ironing it with a cool iron until dry, placing it in fresh blotting-paper and under a weight for the night, or for at least eight hours.

Avoid placing the blotting-paper to press on a floor made of brick or stone. Rising damp will ruin your plant specimens, which will form mildew and go mouldy. Always check any plant material after a few days, because sometimes just one damp flower will spoil the others. If this does happen, simply remove the offending piece and change the blotting-paper. In an emergency only, tissues and soft napkins can be used instead of blotting-paper; iron them flat before using them. Small items of this type can be placed between the pages of a book with a weight positioned on top. Always pad sharp weights and bricks, since they may damage a book cover, or place a newspaper or magazine between the weight and the book.

When you sort your plant material for drying, take only one variety of flower or leaf at a time; do not mix different sorts. Always try to place types of the same thickness together. Bulky flower heads should be pressed on their own, and the leaves and stems on a separate piece of blotting-paper.

Flower heads are often pressed better head down, but try sideways positions as well to create flower profiles. It is important not to attempt to alter the natural curve of little stems; they are often not straight on the plant, so it is not necessary to make them straight for pressing, and the different shapes will make a design more interesting. Ferns and grasses, both of which press extremely well, have wonderful curved shapes, and they are ideal for large pressed-flower pictures.

YOU WILL NEED

A flower press or sheets of blotting-paper

Weights

Tweezers

Scissors

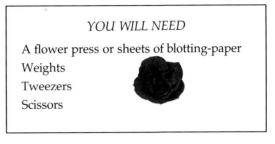

HOW TO POSITION

To press plant material successfully you must first prepare the plants. If you are pressing the whole plant with the flower, stem and leaves, make sure that it will have plenty of space to spread while it dries. First, tidy the stems and take off any leaves that may be brown or damaged. The plant should not protrude beyond the blotting-paper, and ideally, there should be at least an inch (2-3cm) space around the edges of the paper so that the plant is evenly weighted under the press.

If you are drying the heads only, allow sufficient space between each flower, setting them out in neat rows (as illustrated on pages 92-3). Leaves should also be set out in this way, but sometimes, depending on their shape, they can be placed head-to-tail to economize on space.

Mosses, which look unnatural if they are flattened, should be air dried, using a tray or a piece of wire netting. This also applies to seeds, nuts and roots.

Flowers such as carnations, rose buds and sea holly heads, which are rather bulky, can be sliced in half with a sharp craft knife. Both halves can be dried next to each other and used as separate flowers when pressed.

Pressing is often a matter of luck, but as you gain experience, you will find you have great success.

OPPOSITE: pressed leaves: silverweed, mimosa, maple, clematis, fennel, heather, rose, nettle, maidenhair fern, wild rose stem, sea lavender, cineraria, elder, grasses, raspberry leaves, herb robert, artemisia, centurea, juniper, *Berberis thunbergii* 'Aurea', dicentra, *Santolina virens* (syn. *S. rosmarinifolia rosmarinifolia*), asplenium (fern), epimedium, hedge bedstraw, rue, wormwood and pyrethrum.

PICTURE PROJECTS

The equipment needed for pressing flowers and completing the projects: (left, from top to bottom) a selection of cards and papers; (top, from left to right) rulers, labels for identifying pressed flowers, a note book for your records and squares of textured-thread paper; (centre) a flower press; (bottom, from left to right) pressed flowers and a partly begun design, craft knife, glue, orange sticks, black outline pen, pencil sharpener, rubber, pencils, silver and gold outline pens, scissors, tube of rubber-based adhesive and (bottom right) tweezers and pressed plant materials.

Pressed-flower pictures are a stunning way of showing off your hard work. Pictures can be made very simply, or they can be created by using many types of plant material and other accessories to form larger collages. If you are a beginner, start with something small and do not be over-ambitious, and it would be wise to make several different sorts before embarking upon more complicated designs.

It is perfectly possible to improvise with materials you have at home, but if you are seriously considering making a number of items using pressed flowers, there is some equipment you will need to acquire. A large board is extremely useful. You may have limited space to work in, and you can move the board away when you need the area for

something else. I often work on my kitchen table – I like the height and there is excellent light to make my pictures – so obviously, when it comes to preparing a meal, the flowers have to be moved!

A good stock of background papers and card, some sharp scissors, tweezers, a plastic ruler, a pencil, rubber and rubber-based glue are all important. I also like to have several outline pens in black, silver and gold to frame my designs, and drawing pins to secure the paper to the board or card.

Good quality paper is essential, too. If you use a flimsy weight, it will pucker and the glue will seep through, ruining your finished work. Art shops stock some beautiful papers and cards, and it will be well worth buying some heavy watercolour paper, for example, which is wonderful to work on and gives a clean, crisp finish. Stencil card is also excellent since it does not crease easily. Generally, pressed flowers look best on natural colours; deep greens, ambers, shades of brown and grey heighten the effect of the design and give depth to the picture. Patterned paper can be used as well, and faint stripes or soft sponging provide marvellous backgrounds. Fabric is perfect for making the picture seem old fashioned. Velvets, satins, hessian and good cottons look beautiful, and accessories, such as lace and ribbon, can be used to border the picture and to create a soft, romantic feel.

Apart from pressed plant material, you can incorporate many other pretty accessories into your pictures. Sea shells, tiny buttons and beads, sequins and small dried vegetable such as lentils and split peas, can all be used, and sand can be stuck to the base of the picture to create seascapes. In addition although the process is rather lengthy, you can also dry seaweed with some success.

There are two textures of seaweed: the very thin, transparent type, and the thicker, rather lumpy varieties. Rinse thin types at least six times in fresh water to remove unwanted materials and sand and place them on a piece of muslin. Use a paint brush to position the fronds in the most attractive way possible before placing the seaweed in about five layers of blotting-paper, which has to be changed every eight hours for about four days. Then place the papers beneath weights. Bulky types of seaweed should be boiled briefly in salt water and then drained; the pressing process is then the same as for thin types. The Edwardians and Victorians practised this art to perfection, and wonderful pictures can still be found in some antique stores.

FRAMES

Selecting a frame to suit your work can often be a rather overwhelming task as there are so many types to choose from. Over the years I have collected many beautiful frames from second-hand shops, markets and antique stores. These have often surrounded a hideous print, but, once that is removed, they make the most splendid frames for pressed-flower pictures. Some of these frames may be quite plain, but with a little imagination, you can transform them, you

could, for example, try painting the frame to match the colours in your picture. Spray paint is the easiest to use and dries very quickly. Before painting, however, make sure that the frame has been smoothed with sandpaper and there are no protruding nails.

Take care not to use very elaborate, heavy frames that will overpower your design. The work would have to be very large indeed to match this type of frame. It is still possible to find beautiful old frames moulded with gesso, and although they often require some repair, they can be cut down to a reasonable size and look stunning finished in gold or silver. These frames are especially suitable for pictures made on velvet.

Oval and round frames are great favourites of mine. I find they lend a soft, romantic feel to a picture, and they are ideal for framing garlands and bouquets. If your picture has been made using raised material, such as whole rose buds, plump moss, nuts, shells and other pieces that will not lie flat, look out for frames that are quite deep and that have a special ledge for the picture to sit on below the glass. Make sure that petals are not pressed tight against the glass, for if any humidity enters the picture, the condensation may cause the petals to discolour and go mouldy.

Expert picture-framing services will be able to advise you and will have experience in finding the type of frame you are seeking (see page 157).

A selection of frames for pressed-flower projects.

FRAMING YOUR OWN PICTURE

If you have purchased a frame, complete with glass, you will need certain materials to complete the framing.

> ### YOU WILL NEED
>
> The frame and glass
> Hardboard backing cut to size
> Stiff card cut to size
> Strong scissors
> Sticky paper tape
> Paper glue
> Pencil and rubber
> Plastic ruler
> Picture pins
> Small hammer
> Craft knife
> Picture hooks
> Picture cord
> Wall hooks

A good picture-framing shop will provide you with a properly glazed frame, complete with the hardboard backing and a mount, cut to the size you have chosen, and small items such as picture pins, hooks and cord. Art shops stock a range of strong card and glue, and hardware shops usually have picture hooks, hammers and scissors.

MOUNTING YOUR OWN PICTURE

If you wish to make your own mount, you will need the following items to carry out the work with ease.

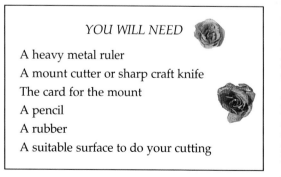

> ### YOU WILL NEED
>
> A heavy metal ruler
> A mount cutter or sharp craft knife
> The card for the mount
> A pencil
> A rubber
> A suitable surface to do your cutting

First, cut the card to fit within the frame as accurately as possible, then work out where you want your picture to be placed.

Experiment by placing it beneath the frame to work out where you wish the mount to begin. Measure this area and lightly mark the places on the reverse side of the card, using the ruler to calculate the exact spacing from the edges of the frame. Join the lines, using faint pencil markings, then place the card on the area on which you are going to do the cutting. Place the mount cutter on the board or use a craft knife (which must be held at a slight angle). Pull the cutter or the knife towards you along the pencil lines, using the heavy ruler as a guide. Turn the card to face you before each line is cut, so that you are always cutting towards you. Press the centre piece of card out of the mount and tidy any edges, then turn the mount the right way round. Purchasing a mount cutter will be necessary only if you will be doing large quantities of this type of work; a knife, although tricky to use, will be more than adequate.

Whether you make your own mount or you have had one especially cut, centre the work, leaving at least 1-2in (3-5cm) of the picture to remain all round under the mount and place a spot of glue on the mount to keep the picture in place.

Even if you have decided not to use a mount, the next stage is the same for both mounted and unmounted designs. First, check that the glass is completely free from grease marks, fingerprints or small objects. Lay the empty frame with the glass side down, and place the picture inside it. The design should not touch the glass but should rest on a small ledge. If there is no ledge, ask your picture framer to make one, which can be simply done by placing a rim of thin wood all round the frame.

After placing the picture on the ledge, put the piece of hard backing card behind it and then the hardboard, which should fit within the frame, leaving the tiniest spaces, so that picture pins can be very gently tapped into place to stop it falling out. The pins should be placed at an angle so that they lie as flat as possible to the hardboard and do not protrude beyond the back of the frame. Then lay sticky tape all round the edge of the frame and hardboard to seal and finish off the framing neatly. Work out the places for the picture hooks and screw them securely into the back of the frame. Tie the picture wire or cord to the hooks and your picture is ready to hang.

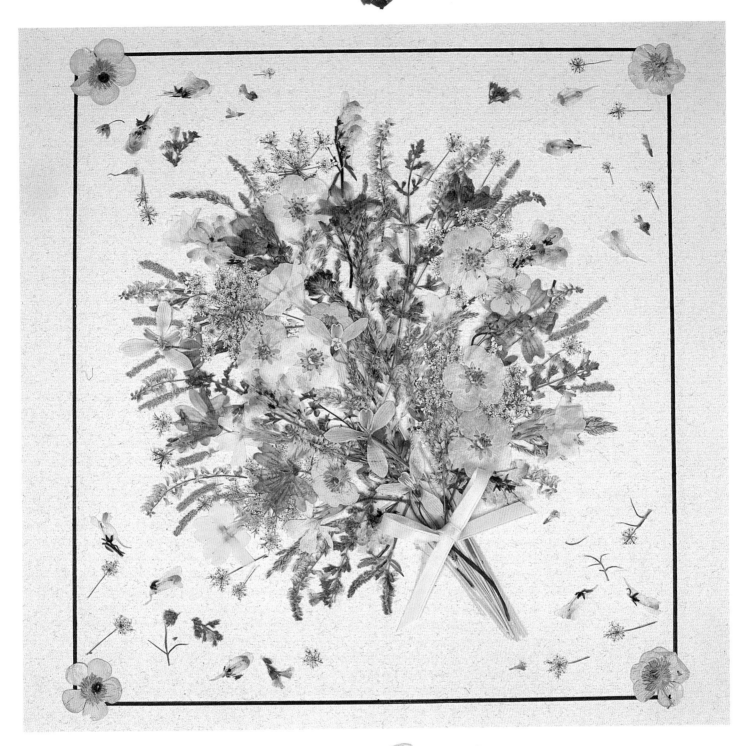

MAKING A PICTURE USING PRESSED FLOWERS

Making a pressed-flower picture cannot be hurried. You will need a great amount of clear space and even more time and patience! Work in good daylight, as night light tends to distort colour and is far more tiring on the eyes. It is extremely important to clear the room of animals: many a picture has been ruined by a wagging tail or affectionate cat.

This spring bouquet was made principally with tamarisk, buttercups, primroses, mallow, cow parsley, grasses, snowdrops, melilot and yellow toadflax.

A cottage garden in summer, a dried-flower picture made from delphiniums, hydrangeas, cosmos, campanula, cow parsley, buttercups, roses, yellow toadflax, tamarisk, cornflowers, heather, pansies, daisies, violas, wild achillea, geraniums, forget-me-nots, alchemilla, achimenes and petunias.

After deciding on the flowers, other plant materials and accessories you are going to use, and then on the prevailing colour of your picture, set the paper or card on your working board and secure it with a drawing pin at each corner. Before you begin to place the flowers, it is useful to make a rough sketch of the picture you wish to make. If you are going to make a circlet of flowers to form a garland, draw a circle very lightly with your pencil on to your paper, using either a compass or by drawing round an object such as a bowl. If you are going to make a swag, heart or other shape, find an appropriate object to draw around to give you a base to work from and prevent you from making errors of shape and proportion.

Take each flower in turn, using tweezers if desired, and begin with the central part of your design. If you are using whole stems, complete with the flowers and leaves, place these on first so that you can see the different shapes. Don't be afraid to cut leaves and flowers in half or to extract petals to use in the design. You can even invent plants with the materials you have. Fill in the spaces with the other flowers and leaves until you are happy with the picture.

I often leave the room at this stage and return after 20 minutes. I find that, with

The autumn garland contains a mixture of pressed leaves and flowers including bramble leaves, pansy leaves, hydrangeas, rose of Sharon, daisies, wild roses, freesias, alchemilla, kerria, raspberry leaves, beech leaves, celandines and elecampane (elfwort).

fresh eyes, I can quickly see any alterations that I want to make before I stick the pieces down. If you wish to make a border, do this before going on to the next stage. You should then prepare to stick the flowers to the paper. You will need the orange sticks and the glue. Always keep the glue on a plate or saucer or you will find that little bits stick to everything else and you get into a terrible mess.

There are two ways of sticking flowers to

paper. One way is to begin at the bottom and work up; alternatively, you can turn the paper as you work. It is not necessary to glue everything perfectly the first time round, just stick down the centres of the flowers and leaves. The important thing is to get each piece stuck in position. You can glue down all the remaining petals when you have completed this. Do not use too much glue – the tiniest amount, placed on an orange stick will suffice – and any excess can usually be

rolled away when it is completely dry.

Make sure that you glue all the stems securely, snipping off any pieces that are in the way or are preventing a flower from lying quite flat. If you are making a dense collage picture of the kind shown on pages 102-3, you should glue all the material nearest to the paper first, then stick the other plants to these.

Let the glue dry for about 15 minutes, then place a piece of paper over your work, place it on a flat surface and cover it with some heavy books to press all the material flat on to the paper and to encourage the glue to stick securely. Leave it under the books overnight, and then your design will be ready for framing.

The winter basket contains a selection of purple larkspur, lawn daisies, hydrangeas, grasses, silverweed, wild rose buds, violas, cow parsley and borage.

OTHER PRESSED-FLOWER PROJECTS

Some of the greetings cards that can be made with pressed flowers.

Making pictures is only one way of using pressed flowers. You can also use them to make greetings cards, bookmarks, place-settings and finger-plates for doors, or you can use them on objects such as boxes of either wood or cardboard, papier mâché plates and bowls and lampshades – in fact, on almost any surfaces you might like to decorate. An experienced designer might enjoy creating a collage on a screen or decorating a wooden table, which would then be covered with glass. Projects like these, however, take much thought and care and should not be undertaken in haste.

GREETINGS CARDS

Everyone loves receiving a card or present especially made by the sender. It is a lovely way of showing that you have thought especially about them, and these cards and presents can be kept and treasured as wonderful keepsakes.

Greetings cards need not be large; small cards are, in fact, usually more practical to send, and you will find it easier to buy matching envelopes. Designs can be very simple: a few flowers made into a small posy or a pattern running around the card to

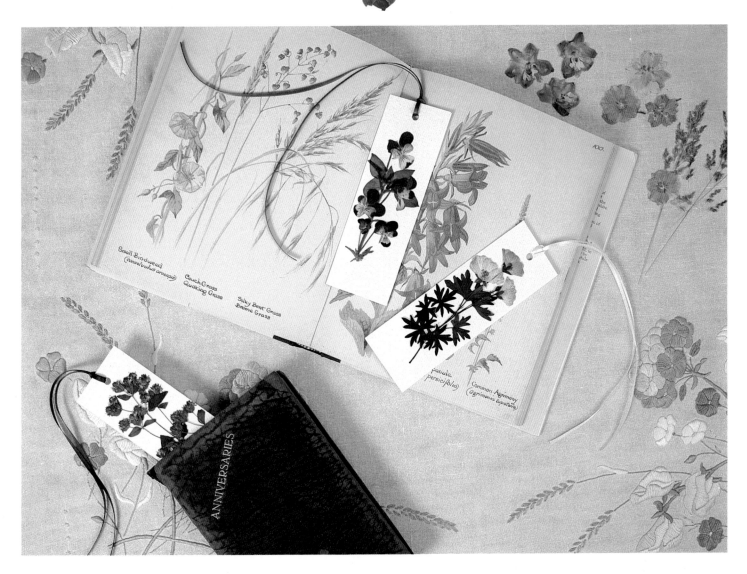

YOU WILL NEED

The same items as for making a pressed-flower picture (see pages 101-5) plus some clear film to cover the finished card

serve as a border for a small central picture are ideal for this type of card. The method is exactly the same as for a pressed-flower picture except that everything is on a smaller scale. You must use good quality paper that is strong and will stand up easily when it has been folded in half.

Cut the piece of card or good quality stiff paper to size, bearing in mind that it will be folded in half. If you are planning to make many cards, it might be wise to work out a size then buy a pack of matching envelopes. When you have cut the paper to size, this is the best moment to make a border, since a mistake with an outline pen once the flowers

are firmly stuck to the paper would be disastrous. Use the finest pen possible; if you do want a wider line, make sure that the pen is not 'fluffy' as this will cause the lines to blur.

Next work out your design and glue it to the card. Make sure all the little pieces are firmly stuck down, then wait a while for the glue to dry. Place a piece of paper over the card and leave it under a heavy book for about an hour. Remove the paper and book, then measure sufficient transparent film to fit exactly over the card. Most rolls of film are made on backing paper printed with squares to help with the measuring. Working from the top of the card, unpeel the first part of the prepared film and place it very carefully on your design. Press this part down, then holding the card, unpeel the film little by little, until the whole design is covered. You should always smooth it as you go to prevent air bubbles forming. Trim any excess

Bookmarks made with pressed flowers and decorated with pretty ribbons.

YOU WILL NEED

Very heavy paper or card

Pressed plant materials

Scissors

Craft knife

Transparent ruler

Rubber-based glue

Orange sticks

Pencil

Rubber

Outline pen (optional)

Transparent film (bookmarks only)

12in (30cm) narrow ribbon

A glass or plastic finger-plate and screws (finger-plate only)

Screwdriver (for attaching the finger-plate to a door)

A finger-plate (left) made with pressed cranesbill and (right) one made with a design of pressed pansies

Using the stiff paper or card, cut narrow rectangular strips to the size you require. Bookmarks can be as long or short as you wish, but the card for the finger-plates will have to be measured to keep it to the exact outer edge proportions of the glass or plastic cover. Work out the designs you wish to make, trying to avoid placing pressed materials on the very edges of the card. The designs could be made within a border, or you could place flowers at random.

Before you begin the bookmark, make a mark at the base of the card where you will punch a hole to place a ribbon. The glass or plastic finger-plates will already have holes at the top and bottom, so make pencil rings on the card to show where to punch the holes. When you have completed the picture, check that all the materials are secure. Place some transparent film over the bookmark (see Greetings Cards for method) to protect it. Then punch a hole through the card and the seal where you made your pencil mark. Fold the ribbon in half and knot it through the hole.

Finger-plates can be mounted directly behind the glass or plastic surround. Make holes in the door, then secure the finger-plate in position using the screws provided. Special screws with rounded heads are available for this type of fixture, and they look far more attractive.

film from the sides and place the card again under the paper and books to settle the film.

Place-settings are made in exactly the same way, except they are tiny. You will not necessarily have to cover them with film either unless you are planning to use them again and again.

BOOKMARKS AND FINGER-PLATES

Both bookmarks and finger-plates are made in the same way, the only difference being that they are different sizes and the finger-plates do not require transparent film as they are placed under glass or clear plastic. Both make wonderful presents, and the bookmarks are fun and easy for a child to undertake.

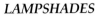

LAMPSHADES

If you are thinking of decorating a lamp-shade, you can either buy a ready-made shade or you can attempt to make your own shade and then decorate it. Ready-made shades are far simpler to handle if you are a beginner, and it is a good idea to practise picture making on some ready-made shades before attempting to make your own. Buy a plain, strong paper shade, preferably in a light colour, as the light will shine through the flowers in a prettier way. Use flowers that are not too bulky or dense in colour to give an impression of transparency. Petunias, irises and pansies look very pretty, and you could try adding some leaves that are either fern shapes or of a type such as clematis, which give a trailing effect. Grasses look particularly stunning on lampshades.

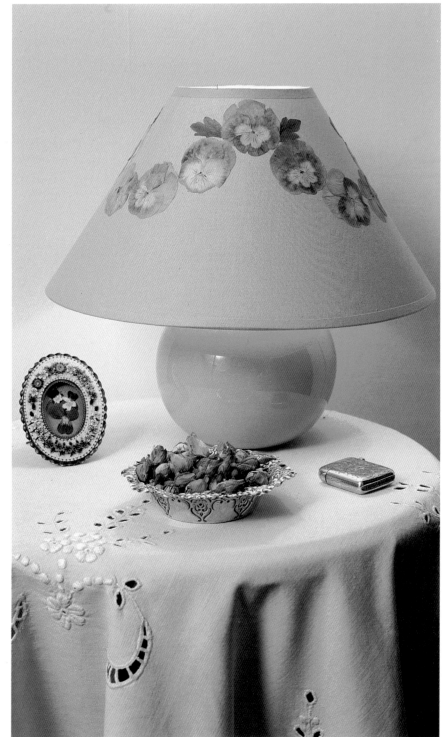

YOU WILL NEED

A lampshade

Pressed flowers

Rubber-based glue (and a plate or saucer)

Orange sticks

Scissors

Tweezers

Craft knife

I find the easiest way to decorate a shade is to hold it in my lap and turn it as I work. Remember that at the half-way point you have to take care not to knock the flowers that are already in place. It is also easy to work with the shade on a table below you.

Holding the shade on its side, plan the design you want to make. Swags often look pretty and can be created from the top or bottom rim. It is helpful to work out a design on a piece of paper before you begin.

Using a minimal amount of glue, stick only the outer points of the petals and leaves. If you use too much glue it will show through the shade. Work around the shade to complete your design, occasionally holding it to the light to check the effect of the flowers and the design you are making. If it is a repeat design, you will need to mark the length of the pattern repeat with a pencil on the shade so that you do not overlap the pattern at the starting point.

When the shade is finished, it will need to be covered to protect the flowers. Although it is possible to cover it with transparent film, I would recommend taking it to a photographic laboratory where it could be laminated. This is an excellent process, which will not only make the shade look professional but will properly seal all the flower material to the shade.

A lampshade decorated with a swag design of pressed pansies.

Wooden boxes decorated with tiny pressed flowers, then sealed and varnished.

If the box is wood, sand it down so that there are no pits or scratches; the wood must be completely smooth before you begin. Dust the box and, if you wish to paint it, use either a paint that is suitable for wood or, if it is cardboard, a water-based paint. I often also use water-based paints for wooden boxes, mixing the colours so that they are very watery, then painting the wood to create a stained effect rather than a dense colour. A gold finish on wood can also be attractive, making it look rather antique. I usually paint the inside of the box as well, but you might prefer to line the interior with a pretty paper or fabric.

When the paint is dry, work out the design for your pressed materials. If you are working in a circle, use a pencil to mark the position very lightly.

Place the flowers on the box and, when you are satisfied with the effect, glue them firmly down. Make quite sure there are no loose petals or leaves, or they will lift when the next stage begins, then leave the pressed materials dry for two or three hours or even overnight. The next stage is to seal the flowers. Use a clear-drying PVA adhesive mixed with a little water or one of the specially prepared solutions. This must be painted on and left to dry before you varnish; it is important not to miss out this stage or the varnish will spoil the flowers. Dust the box gently before varnishing. Use a clear picture varnish and apply five or six coats, making sure that each coat is completely dry before applying the next. Check that no hairs from the brush are shed on to the surface, and always dust the surface before applying the next coat. While you are applying the varnish, always go round the edges of the box with a dry brush to stop any drip marks forming.

When you have applied all the coats, check that there are no runs or lumps. If you find any imperfections, use fine sandpaper to smooth them away, and then apply another coat. If you feel that six coats are not enough, apply several more. The greater the protection, the better.

DECORATING BOXES WITH PRESSED FLOWERS

Boxes decorated with pressed flowers look simply beautiful. They can be used to house jewellery, special letters or just odds and ends! Any type of box can be used, but my own favourites are cigar boxes, which are usually quite well made, particularly if the cigars were the huge, expensive sort! You can also decorate the stiff cardboard gift-type boxes and make them look equally stunning.

YOU WILL NEED

A box

Sandpaper

Paint

Glue

Sealing agent

Varnish

Pressed plant materials

Scissors

Tweezers

Rubber-based glue

Pencil and rubber

Orange sticks

Craft knife

DECORATING PAPIER MACHÉ

Papier mâché is very easy and very inexpensive to make. You can make several things at once, and they are great fun to decorate and use as ornaments at home or give away as attractive, imaginative gifts.

YOU WILL NEED

A quantity of newspaper

Wallpaper adhesive and a medium width brush

A pot of Vaseline

A wide-rimmed bowl, plate or dish

Scissors

For the decoration

Acrylic paint

Pressed plant materials

Rubber-based glue (in a plate or saucer)

Orange sticks

Scissors

Tweezers

Plastic sealant

First, find an interestingly shaped open bowl or dish. It is best to start with something simple, and a salad bowl is ideal.

Tear or cut masses of newspapers into strips. Magazines are also useful but should be used only after a quantity of the newspaper has been applied first. Rub Vaseline over the inside of the bowl or plate, making sure that it is coated thinly all over, right up to the rim and slightly over it.

Wet the first strips of paper with a little water, and mould them to the bottom of the bowl, smoothing them down so that there are no air bubbles. Each strip should overlap the last, and they should be brought right up and over the rim (they can be trimmed afterwards). Place the next layer on top of the first, using the wallpaper paste made up according to the instructions on the packet. Put three layers on altogether, and leave to dry for at least 24 hours; sometimes it will be necessary to leave it longer. When dry, build up the next layers until there are at least twelve. If you do fewer, the result will be too flimsy. When all the layers have dried properly, edge the shape out of the mould and tidy the edges. The Vaseline should

have prevented any of the paper sticking to the base of the mould. Make sure that there are no gaps, where the paper is not sufficiently well stuck down, then take an acrylic paint, mix the colour you have chosen and paint the bowl.

When the paint is dry and you have created the colours and effects you wish, you can prepare the pressed plant materials to go in position. When you have worked out the design, glue the flowers to the surface using a little rubber-based glue. Make sure each piece is stuck down firmly. When the glue is dry, apply a sealant (see Decorating Boxes for method) over the plants and let it dry. Then apply six coats of varnish on both the top and the underside of the bowl or dish, dusting the surfaces before each coat is applied.

A papier mâché vase can be made in the same way, except you cover the outside of the container with paper. When the stages are complete, cut down neatly through the paper and then glue the two halves together, using a very strong paper glue.

It is possible to create many textures with papier mâché. You could, for example, place a layer of fine muslin over the bowl and glue it to the surface before painting; or you could use different widths of different papers, cut into shapes and stuck down to form a pattern. You can have hours of fun and produce some wonderful results.

A papier mâché plate and pot, both decorated with pressed flowers, then sealed and varnished.

PAGES 112-13: some of the ingredients for winter pot pourri, which is described on pages 140-1.

POT POURRI

Pot pourri has been with us for centuries, although not always in the form with which are familiar today. Records show that the Egyptians were the first to use herbs, spices and flowers to make essences and balms. The balms were for healing and annointing, and fragrant essences were burned as offerings to their gods. The Egyptians carried flower petals about with them to provide fragrance in the same way we use perfume. The floors of banqueting halls and palaces were strewn with fresh rose petals, and linen was washed with flower-scented water. Today we rely more on chemically scented washing powders, which may be effective but do not have the charm of by-gone times. The wonderful fragrances that were used in the past, however – sandalwood, ambergris, frankincense and myrrh, gillyflowers and rose petals, for instance – are still used for scenting modern pot pourri.

The Greeks learned about perfume from the Egyptians, and vast quantities of petals were shipped to Greece, to be used in much the same way as in Egypt. The Greeks passed on their knowledge to the Romans, and, as the Roman Empire extended its frontiers, perfume spread to the rest of Europe. Research into perfumes continued to be carried out, and the value of herbs in particular increased with the discovery of their healing properties. The Greeks recorded their findings, the first known manuscript dating from the first century AD. This manuscript was translated, and copies adapted from the original texts could be found as late as the thirteenth century. It was the Arabs, however, who revolutionized the art of perfumery by separating plant extracts into oils, and they worked particularly with the one we use so much today, the rose, the basis of so many modern perfumes.

Throughout the centuries these fragrances became widely used by Europeans, and in Elizabethan times the mistress of the house had a still-room, a room near the kitchen where she made her own potions from herbs to keep her household healthy. She would also create floral fragrances for her home, strewing herbs on the floors to refresh the air and making little bags filled with herbs to scent clothes and linen. It was not, however, until the eighteenth century that the word pot pourri was used to describe the familiar mixes of scents that we use now. The words

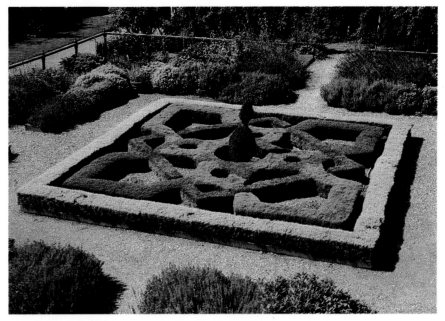

pot pourri literally mean 'rotten pot', and the mixes were more commonly made using a moist method (see pages 130-1).

From Elizabethan times the area devoted to herbs was virtually the most important place in the garden. Although herb gardens were entirely functional, many were designed in the most elaborate fashion. Networks of little individual plots were encircled with pathways or low-growing hedges that divided the areas into geometrical designs around a central point, which would be a statue, a fountain or a pond. The paths were not only created for decorative purposes but they served to prevent one type of herb spreading into another, so keeping the garden tidy and controlling the size of the plants. These gardens were usually near to the kitchen entrance of the house for purely practical reasons, and that is an excellent hint for anyone thinking of creating a herb garden, for it can be unpleasant to have to collect herbs from the very bottom of the garden when it is dark or pouring with rain.

Flower gardens were designed in much the same way, with picturesque areas displaying masses of roses, which were then, as they still are, very much the centre of attention. These flower gardens were also geometrically designed, and were usually surrounded with neat little box hedges.

A formally laid out knot garden.

OPPOSITE: a linen cupboard fragranced with perfumed sachets, lavender bottles and pomanders.

MAKING YOUR OWN POT POURRI

These baskets of garden flowers that have been gathered for drying contain yellow and orange zinnia heads and, in the larger basket, alchemilla, achillea 'Moonshine', achillea 'The Pearl', helipterum (acroclinium) daisies, larkspurs, marjoram, rudbeckia, sea lavender and santolina (cotton lavender).

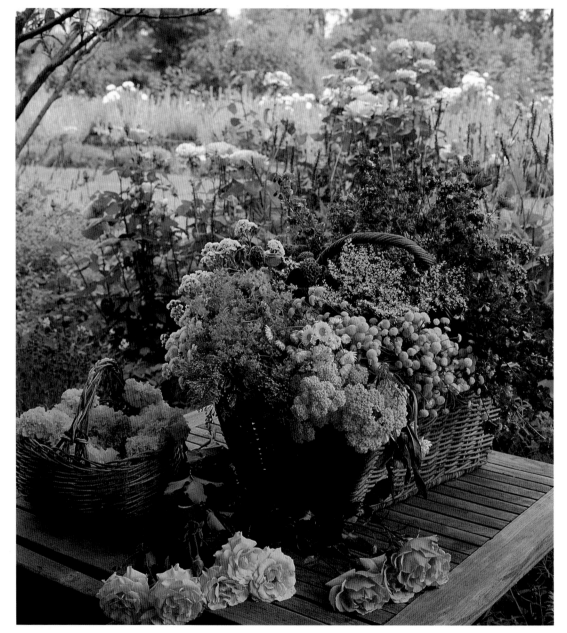

Pot pourri has a nostalgic quality of its own. I have often walked into a room and wondered what the wonderful scent is, sometimes a musky fragrance, sometimes a perfume reminiscent of summer gardens, and then my eye is caught by a colourful bowl of pot pourri.

If it is made correctly, pot pourri can be fragrant for a very long time. This is especially so if you make it yourself, adding the perfumes that you love. There are some beautiful mixes of pot pourri available commercially, but I often find them disappointing as the scent does not remain and the flowers quickly fade. There are, of course, several quality makers, some of which are listed on page 157, and they will usually be able to supply you with petals and oils to add to your own mixes. I think however, it is far nicer and more rewarding to create your own blends, and it really is one of the most satisfying ways to preserve flowers and herbs from your own garden. A garden does not have to be very big to provide the quantity of flowers you will need for making several bowls.

A FLOWER GARDEN FOR POT POURRI

Today, the floral garden has become more popular than ever, and gardening enthusiasts spend enormous amounts of time and effort in creating exquisite floral displays of every type and colour. Colour is one of the most important elements for a visually pretty bowl of pot pourri, and in addition to the many highly scented flowers you will require, there are many unscented varieties you can use for purely decorative purposes.

Some flowers, of course, have both wonderful scent and colour, but others, not so highly scented, are important to make your mix look original and attractive. Among the flowers that are perfect for this purpose are larkspur and delphiniums, which do not smell particularly sweet when dry but whose petals retain excellent colour, expecially the blue varieties, which can be quite vivid. The flowers of everlasting statice are also unscented but are so useful for adding colour and bulk. There are many other flowers you can use, and some of these are given on this page, divided into two lists, one for scented and one for unscented.

Foliage is also important for adding fragrance, and some plants have especially pungent leaves. These include hypericum, scented geranium, olearia, juniper and pine, not to mention the dozens of fragrant herbs that are listed later in this chapter.

ROSES

The rose, the most romantic flower of all, is such a special flower: its appeal is endless, and even after all these centuries it is still one of the most vital ingredients for many floral mixes. Many roses can be grown for their fragrance, and their long flowering seasons give us an opportunity to accumulate a good stock of petals. Some rose shrubs flower only once during the summer, but even then a mature bush can grow to spectacular heights and produce numerous blooms.

SCENTED	UNSCENTED
Carnation	Achillea
Daphne	Alchemilla
Flowering tobacco (Nicotiana)	Chrysanthemum
Hibiscus	Coreopsis
Honeysuckle	Cornflower
Hyacinth	Cosmos
Jasmine	Delphinium
Lavender	Golden rod
Lily-of-the-valley	Gypsophila
Meadowsweet	Heather
Night-scented stock	Hydrangea
Mignonette	Larkspur
Peony	Malva
Pink	Marigold
Rose	Pansy
Stephanotis	Statice
Stock	Tree mallow
Syringa	Tulip
Vibernum	Zinnia
Violet	
Wallflower	

There are so many varieties of rose that it would be impossible to list them all, but here are some of the varieties that you might try growing. You will not need them all – indeed, two or three varieties will suffice. The roses described are excellent not just for their appearance but also for their extraordinary fragrance.

ALBA

Alba roses range in colour from white, through blush, to pink. 'Cuisse de Nymphe' is a pretty rose, which grows to about 6ft (1.8m). It is also sometimes called 'Great Maiden's Blush'. The flowers are the palest pink, and the perfume is exquisite, but it has a short flowering season of only three weeks. 'Queen of Denmark' ('Königin von Dänemark') is a classic pink rose with an overwhelmingly strong scent. It grows to 5ft (1.5m).

BOURBON

Fully double blooms are borne by this group of vigorous growers. 'Mme Isaac Pereire' can grow to 7ft (2.1m). It produces deep pink flowers with an extraordinary scent, which

appear throughout most of the summer. 'Bourbon Queen' is a great favourite for cottage garden walls, and it can grow to 10ft (3m). The cupped-shaped flowers are pink and magenta. 'La Reine Victoria' grows to 6ft (1.8m). The deep pink, highly scented blooms are borne throughout the whole summer and into autumn.

DAMASK

Although most Damask roses bloom only once each summer, the group includes some of the most beautiful roses of all. 'Celsiana' grows to 6ft (1.8m), and its deliciously scented blooms, which are brilliant pink, appear for most of the summer. 'Mme Hardy' flowers from mid-summer and will reach a height of nearly 7ft (2.1m). It has stunning, perfectly formed, brilliant white blooms and the most delightful scent.

GALLICA

Suitable for hedging as well as for planting in borders, Gallica roses tend to flower only once, although some varieties do bear a second flush of blooms in the autumn. 'Belle de Crécy' grows to 4ft (1.2m) and has wonderful purple-red blooms, which mature to violet with a green button centre, from mid-summer. 'Cardinal de Richelieu' grows to 4ft (1.2m) and has double, pale pink flowers, which eventually turn to a violet-purple, from mid-summer.

HYBRID PERPETUAL

There are no yellow Hybrid Perpetuals, but the colours available within this group range from the deepest maroon to pink and white. 'Général Jacqueminot' grows to 4ft (1.2m) and has very strongly scented, double blooms of deep crimson. 'Mrs John Laing' is a very pretty pink rose with double blooms, which appear from early summer into autumn. It will grow to 5ft (1.5m).

RUGOSA

Almost all Rugosa roses are fragrant, but they are, on the whole, rather prickly – so wear your gardening gloves. 'Agnes' has sweetly fragrant, rich yellow, double flowers, which are pompon shaped and which appear early in the season, with some later flowering as well. It will grow to a height of about 6ft (1.8m). 'Sarah van Fleet' grows to

Some brilliantly coloured roses, collected for drying so that they can be used in the making of pot pourri.

8ft (2.4m) and produces masses of richly scented, pink flowers until late summer.

HYBRID SWEETBRIAR

The free-flowering shrubs in this group are, unfortunately, rather prone to mildew, but if you are prepared to spray to combat this, the blooms will prove a delight. 'Amy Robsart' grows to about 6ft (1.8m) and has semi-double, rich rose-pink blooms, which appear in mid-summer. In autumn the bush will often have masses of rose hips, which are useful for decorating pot pourri.

MOSS

This group of roses gets it name from the bristles, sometimes hard and spiny, sometimes soft and fur-like, that cover the calyx, flower stems or the leaves. 'Mme Delaroche-Lambert' is a beautiful rose, which bears semi-double flowers of vivid rose-purple. It will grow to 4ft (1.2m) and flowers at intervals right through to autumn. 'Henri Martin' bears semi-double, vivid crimson flowers with white midribs. It will grow to 5ft (1.5m)

PORTLAND

Roses in this group flower intermittently throughout summer and into autumn. 'Compte de Chambord' is a rose with delicious scent and dense pink petals. It flowers all summer and grows to 4ft (1.2m).

CENTIFOLIA

These hardy roses are often known as cabbage roses. 'Tour de Malakoff' will grow to 6ft (1.8m), bearing blooms of an extraordinary magenta colour, which turns to grey-violet when mature, in mid-summer.

HYBRID TEA

There are so many varieties of Hybrid Tea (or large-flowered bush roses, as they are now known) that are suitable for growing that I have listed them by colour. These roses are not only highly scented but are ideal for drying to include in displays and bouquets. Red: 'Ena Harkness' and 'Josephine Bruce'; pink: 'Bonsoir' and 'Admiral Rodney'; yellow: 'Golden Times', 'King's Ransom' and 'Peer Gynt'; white: 'Message'; lilac: 'Blue Moon'; and orange: 'Alexander' and 'Fred Gibson'.

CLIMBING OR RAMBLING

If you have some wall space, a pillar, a trellis or a fence, the following roses will look stunning trained against it. 'Crimson Glory', a wonderful plant, grows to 10-12ft (3-3.6m) and has velvet crimson flowers in mid-summer. 'Emily Gray' is a vigorous rambler, which will reach heights of 10ft (3m). The wonderfully scented flowers are a rich gold. 'New Dawn' will flower almost continuously throughout the summer bearing silvery pink blooms. It is ideal to train up a pillar and can grow to 9ft (2.7m) 'Sanders White Rambler' is a stunning rose to grow as an arch. It

has double white, highly scented blooms, which appear in early summer. It grows to an incredible 12-15ft (3.6-4.5m). 'Zéphirine Drouhin' has carmine pink, double flowers, which are borne until late autumn. If supported it will grow to 9ft (2.7m).

LAVENDER

Lavender is used almost as much as the rose in the making of pot pourri. Its refreshing perfume has a special quality that lends both fragrance and colour. The variety 'Hidcote' has deep purple-blue flowers and 'Hidcote Pink' bears pinkish blooms, and

both varieties are shorter stemmed – growing to 2-3ft (60-90cm) – than some of the varieties more often seen in English gardens. The stems of the variety 'Grappenhall' will grow up to 4ft (1.2m) with each head measuring 2-3in (5.7cm). The foliage is a greyer blue than that of 'Hidcote', and is ideal for making lavender bottles (see pages 148-50). If you do not already have a lavender bush, it would be advisable to purchase several to obtain a good harvest in the first year. Sometimes garden centres have quite mature bushes for sale, which are an excellent acquisition, as they take several years to become established and grow tall.

'Hidcote', one of the most deliciously fragrant varieties of lavender.

Rose petals, larkspur florets, cotton lavender and marigolds placed in slatted containers ready for sorting.

GATHERING AND DRYING FLOWERS FOR POT POURRI

Flowers can be dried for pot pourri in exactly the same way as flowers for displays (see pages 28-32), but some flowers – roses, marigolds, peonies and sunflowers, for instance – benefit from having their petals stripped before drying, especially when you simply require them for bulk. Little rose buds should be dried whole, since their petals are too small for this purpose, and they can also be used for surface decoration. Choose flower heads that are in full bloom, leaving the other, tighter flowers for air drying or for treatment by the silica gel method.

are ideal for this purpose. Turn the petals after a couple of days, and then turn them again every so often until they are completely dry. They should feel crisp and warm when they are ready.

You can also dry petals and small flowers using the oven method, which is very quick and useful if you need them immediately. The oven should be on the lowest setting, and individual petals will normally take no longer than 15 or 20 minutes and will make your kitchen smell wonderful!

When air drying whole bunches of flowers, fasten a paper bag over the heads of types that tend to drop such as lavender to catch the florets, which can all be incorporated into pot pourri. Similarly, when you are preparing fresh flowers for drying, any petals and florets that are shed can be dried using the tray method described above, or you can carefully press the petals or flower heads and preserve them for other types of decoration.

When the petals are completely dry, you should store them in airtight glass jars or tins. Plastic containers are not advisable: during warm weather they tend to sweat, which can cause the petals to go mouldy.

A HERB GARDEN FOR POT POURRI

Herbs are not only remarkable for their medicinal and culinary uses but they are also extremely attractive and exude the most enormous range of simply wonderful, bewitching smells. They are also the perfect addition to pot pourri. The range of fragrance is vast, varying as it does from heady, musky aromas to sweet citric and spicy scents.

If you are planning to plant a herb garden from scratch, choose an area as close as possible to the house. Herbs play a vital role in the making of pot pourri, and many are relatively easy to grow. Some herbs, tansy and alkanet, for example, grow wild in the countryside. Tansy dries particularly well, the soft, flat clusters of florets retaining a good mustard yellow, while the brilliant little blue flowers of alkanet can be found along hedgerows, visible among the greenery. Wild achillea (yarrow) can be seen growing everywhere during the late summer months, and its flat white or pale pink heads make it easily recognizable. Marshmallow, which grows in wet meadows and along river beds,

When stripping flowers, discard any petals with brown edges or obvious flaws such as insect damage. Lay the petals out on trays, placing them in layers no more than two deep, or the layers underneath will remain damp and rot. Keep the petals in a warm, well-ventilated place out of direct light; a warm, dark cupboard or underneath a bed

Some of the herbs and spices that can be used to add texture to pot pourri.

has the most delicate pink flowers. In warmer Mediterranean countries, rosemary and sage grow in profusion, rosemary particularly liking areas near the sea.

When you begin, experiment with a manageable number of basic herbs, adding some different ones to your garden each year. Ask your nursery for advice on spacing and your garden's soil type before buying too many plants. Divide the plot you mean to cultivate into small areas, perferably separating them by narrow paths or edging them individually with stones to prevent the herbs from growing into each other. It will also make weeding easier. If you do not possess a garden but have a small area outside, you could try growing herbs in tubs or in large terraccotta pots.

Most herbs are perennials and will conveniently reappear each year once they are established. There are a few popular annuals,

however, which have to be planted each spring. These include basil, dill, summer savoury and sweet marjoram. It is best to buy herbs in the form of seedlings, as this will not only save you time but also allow you to choose ones that have already developed into larger plants. Take great care to select only the healthiest looking plants; make sure there are no yellowing leaves or signs of blight. If you are searching for rosemary, buy the biggest plant possible, for it takes ages to become large enough to use. You may not be able to use the plant at all in the first year, but dried rosemary is readily available from most grocers and in health food shops.

If you want to grow your own plants from seed, begin in early spring by sowing seeds in trays or propagators, planting out the seedlings when the weather has improved and there is no further risk of ground frost.

The area should have been well weeded in advance and any large stones removed. Watch out for slugs and snails – they can eat through your entire crop during the night, and they particularly enjoy young seedlings! Most herbs require plenty of sunshine and regular watering, and they will wilt quickly if not attended to daily. Once established, however, some herbs, rosemary, thyme and sage, for instance, will thrive even in very dry conditions, but others, such as mint, bergamot, nasturtiums and sweet cicely, prefer semi-shade and damp earth.

GATHERING AND DRYING HERBS FOR POT POURRI

Herbs for pot pourri should be gathered on a sunny day, when they are at their peak and the leaves are lush and firm. Some plants – rosemary and bay, for example, which thrive all the year round – can be gathered whenever you need them, although the fresh, new leaves of bay are a brighter, lighter green when quite young.

Herbs can be dried in exactly the same way as flowers. They should be picked when they are completely free from dew or rain and be cut with stems that are as long as possible. Place them in a little water while you sort them into bunches as some types wilt quickly, and this will allow you to take your time over selecting the best stems for drying. Herbs should be air dried by hanging them upside down in small bunches in a warm, dry, well-ventilated area out of direct light. Do not hang your herbs to dry in the sun; they will quickly shrivel, become discoloured and lose their charming fragrance.

Herbs take anything from three days to a week or more to dry, depending on the thickness of the foliage. You should fasten a paper bag over the heads of some types, such as thyme and rosemary and those with fine or needly leaves, to catch any dropping leaves. When they are completely dry, store your herbs in airtight containers that have been thoroughly washed and dried before use – large storage jars are perfect for this purpose – and then place them in a cupboard in the dark. Label each jar carefully with the name of the herb and the date it was dried. If you are unfamiliar with herbs it is easy to forget which is which when the plants have been stripped down.

HERBS TO GROW FOR POT POURRI

The herbs listed here are those you might try growing to use in your own pot pourri; the ones marked with an asterisk are the basic herbs, which you could try in the first year. A number of herb farms from which you can obtain plants are given on page 157. Many of these herbs – artemisia, marjoram, bay and sage, for example – are also excellent for use in dried-flower displays and bouquets.

Alkanet (dyer's bugloss)

Anise, star

Apium (lesser marshwort)

Basil

Bay*

Bergamot*

Chamomile, double-flowered

Coriander

Cotton lavender (santolina)*

Costmary (alecost, balsamita)

Curry plant (*Helichrysum angustifolium*)

Hops*

Hyssop

Lemon verbena*

Lovage*

Marjoram, sweet

Marshmallow

Melissa (lemon balm)

Mint, eau-de-Cologne (*Mentha citrata*)*

Myrtle

Nasturtium

Rosemary*

Sage, red (*Salvia officinalis* 'Purpurea')

Sage, variegated (*Salvia icterina*)

Sage, white (*Artemisia ludoviciana*)*

Southernwood (*Artemisia abrotanum*)*

Spearmint (*Mentha spicata*)*

Sweet cicely*

Thyme*

Wormwood (*Artemisia absinthium*)

Yarrow (*Achillea millefolium*)

PRESERVING AND FRAGRANCING POT POURRI

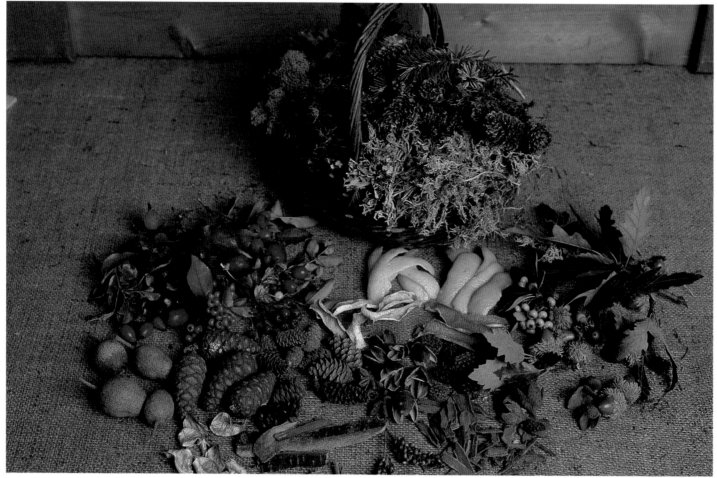

A collection of some of the more unusual ingredients that can be included in pot pourri – moss, cones, berries, bark and citrus peel.

FIXATIVES

Ground herbs, flower petals, roots and mosses are all essential in the creation of successful pot pourri, but without a fixative, the perfume will not endure, so special herbs and spices are used for this purpose. The fixative absorbs the highly scented flower oils that are added to the blends and allows the pot pourri to retain its fragrance, and, with their own exotic and individual scents, they leave your pot pourri fragrant and long lasting.

The commonest fixatives are coarse salt, orris-root and gum benzoin. These are by far the easiest fixatives to come by, and most herablist or health food shops should carry a reasonable supply. (See page 156 for suppliers.)

Cinnamon and cloves are also effective for fixing pot pourri, and you probably already have some in your kitchen. Spices of all types are available from your local grocery store or supermarket, although you may need more than one of the small jars in which they are sold, especially if you are making large quantities. Many highly scented spices can be used for adding a special aroma to pot pourri. Particularly pungent are coriander, cardamom, allspice, nutmeg and the deliciously fragrant vanilla pod, which will add the sweetest aroma.

ESSENTIAL OILS

Essential oils are made by using extracts from flowers, herbs, leaves and woods. The range of different types is enormous: there

126

are sweet, floral fragrances, heady, exotic spicy scents and perfumes from the essences of bark and citrus fruits. Although essential oils are relatively easy to make, the process is quite lengthy as it involves soaking the plant materials in pure oil to extract the fragrance and healing properties.

Many excellent oils are available commercially, and to save time when your flower petals are ready for use. I would suggest you purchase the few that you will need (see below). Several oils are used more frequently than others – rose, lavender, patchouli and lemon verbena seem to be the basis of many classic recipes simply by virtue of their delightful perfumes and the strength of their fragrances. Experiment with several types of rose oil. You will find that rose geranium, damask rose and tea rose all have completely different strengths, and each will suit a different type of recipe.

Essential oils are the purest form of perfume, and they should never be used directly on the skin. They should be mixed with a base oil that has been specially prepared for baths and massage purposes. Their perfumes are extremely strong, and some are quite overpowering when used undiluted, so make sure you follow any recipe carefully.

The list of oils to collect is only a guide and is certainly not definitive; you may have other oils that you have used successfully.

CITRUS FRUITS

The dried rinds of oranges, lemons and limes were used by the ancient Egyptians to make balms and salves, and the fresh, tangy peel is perfect for blending with floral pot pourri and even better for making autumnal fragrances and adding to Christmas recipes.

To prepare the peel correctly, slice very thin pieces from the fruit, taking care not to cut into the pith, which is rather bitter. A small, very sharp vegetable knife or potato peeler is best for this purpose. The peel can be left to dry naturally, placing the pieces on a wire rack or a tray, or it can be dried in a warm, low oven. I find the oven method best, simply from the point of view of time. When the peel is dried, it can be left whole or ground into powder, depending on the effect you wish to achieve.

WOODS, ROOTS, MOSSES, NUTS AND PODS

Many woods and roots have the most aromatic fragrances, and their rather chunky appearance can look splendid combined with other autumn or winter ingredients such as moss, nuts and cones. Apart from the texture, all woods are different colours, ranging from deepest brown to orange. Particularly fragrant are rosewood, sandalwood and cedarwood.

Mosses, resembling soft carpets around the base of tree trunks and clinging to steep banks, can be found in most moist, shady woodlands. There are many different varieties, each with its own colour, ranging from deep, rich green to silver-grey and even yellow. Mosses dry out easily. Place them flat on a wire rack or tray in a warm, well-ventilated area. It is best to wait until they are dry before removing earth and weeds.

Seed heads, pods and cones that appear during late summer and early autumn do not always have strong fragrances, but they can make pot pourri look interesting. Rosehips, fruit kernels, acorns and fir cones become extremely appealing when dry and will give good bulk to woodland mixes.

ESSENTIAL OILS TO COLLECT

Bergamot
Cardamom
Cedarwood
Damask rose
Eucalyptus
Frankincense
Jasmine
Lavender
Lemon verbena
Musk
Myrrh
Narcissus
Neroli
Orange
Patchouli
Rose geranium
Sandalwood
Tea rose
Violet
Ylang-ylang

MAKING POT POURRI

There are two types of pot pourri – moist and dry. Both kinds are easy to make, although moist pot pourri takes longer and is not so visually attractive. It does, however, last for much longer than dry pot pourri, and when ready, it should be placed in especially designed closed jars with small holes perforated in the lid to allow the fragrance to waft gently through into the room.

Dry pot pourri is much quicker to make and is simply stunning to look at. The finished pot pourri can be placed in open bowls, the colours of the flowers enhancing the decor of the room.

DECIDING PROPORTIONS

Before you begin to make your own pot pourri it is important to decide which kind of perfume you like best – is it a sweet floral scent, a spicy, exotic fragrance or a tangy, citric perfume? Although the petals, herbs and spices will influence the aroma, it is the oil you add that will ultimately determine the scent. There are no specific rules on the quantity of oil per volume, and you do not necessarily 'double up' when making larger quantities. Some spices and oils are so powerful that, if used without discretion, they will totally dominate your pot pourri, so great care must be taken in order not to ruin a precious quantity of petals.

The following quantities are for a medium sized bowl of dry pot pourri. They are only a very approximate guide, and you may wish to increase or decrease the proportions according to your own recipes. You may not be able to obtain all the flowers from your own garden, and many spices and oils will have to be obtained from specialist suppliers (see page 156).

YOU WILL NEED

2-4 pints (1-2 litres) flower petals

2oz (60gm) fixative

2-4oz (60-125gm) spices

6 drops of oil

Any other textured ingredients you wish to
    add such as fragranced pods, bark or peel

In time, the scent of your pot pourri will diminish. To revive the fragrance, place all the contents in a waxed paper bag, add half the quantity of the original oils used, a drop of brandy and leave, tightly sealed, for several days, turning the mixture once. Alternatively, there are many excellent ready-prepared pot pourri reviver oils for sale in shops selling pot pourri. These can be found in so many enticing fragrances that you can usually find one that is quite close to your own blend and use this instead.

CONTAINERS

Dry pot pourri can be placed in any type of bowl, dish or basket, while moist pot pourri should be placed in sealed jars with perforated lids. I am always searching in markets, antique shops and junk stores for china bowls and interesting containers with pretty edges or attractive designs around the outside – remember that any interior decoration will be hidden when the dish is filled. Great favourites of mine are old-fashioned cache-pots, which you can sometimes find in the most beautiful shapes, with decorated brims, sides and even handles.

During the eighteenth century some extra-ordinary bowls were made in both England and France. These were made of fine porcelain in very elaborate styles. The containers had perforated lids, which sometimes imitated the design on the bowl, which might have been a leaf or flower pattern. These containers are quite hard to acquire, but they can sometimes be found at specialist antique shops and more frequently at fine art auctions. They are an excellent investment as they are now valuable collector's items and are certainly worth buying if your purse will allow it.

If you decide to use a basket, it is important that you line it first, preferably with either waxed paper or foil. The lining both prevents the petals falling through the weave and protects the basket from being impregnated with oils, which make it unserviceable for any other purpose.

Shining glass bowls are possibly the prettiest containers as you can see all the contents. You could try placing a few

pressed flowers in the bowl first; these will be pressed against the side by the weight of the pot pourri and make the display even more attractive.

If you want a rustic look, terracotta or pottery containers are ideal, and you will probably already have something in your kitchen that would be suitable. Silver bowls will have a grander effect, and they can look stunning, particularly in dining areas where they reflect the silver and glass on the table. I have several highly polished wooden bowls, which look beautiful filled with pot pourri, but the wood does absorb the fragrances, so unless you line the bowls first, you will only be able to use them for this.

Whichever your choice, do avoid leaving bowls of pot pourri in the harsh rays of sunlight, which will make the petals fade very rapidly, leaving rather dull, neutral colours. If you have already made this mistake, you could add some brightly coloured, new petals to the surface of the container.

MOIST POT POURRI

It is said that a moist pot pourri will last for years without requiring any additional ingredient to revive the fragrance. Some have, in fact, been known to last for up to fifty years! So, although the process takes longer and requires far more attention than the making of dry pot pourri, the results are obviously worthwhile. Moist pot pourri is not very attractive to look at, so it is ideal for placing in a container with a perforated lid.

It can take anything from a month up to an entire summer to make moist pot pourri, but it can be made using the simplest ingredients, which will exude the most marvellous perfume when finished. During the preparation, the flower petals will assume a caked appearance, and, eventually, will be ready to mix with oils and herbs to add the final scents. I would suggest that whichever recipe you use, you choose rose petals to form the base; they are not only wonderfully fragrant but are also readily available.

YOU WILL NEED

A large, glazed, terracotta or pottery crock, preferably with straight sides, to hold approximately 8 pints (4 litres)

A plate that will fit inside the crock

A heavy weight to place on the plate

Several long-handled wooden spoons

Coarse, non-iodized rock salt

Flower petals

Herbs and spices

Essential oils

Thin plastic, confectioner's gloves

Several china mixing bowls

A glass eye-dropper

Scales

A length of muslin or gauze to cover the crock

String

The first step is to prepare the flower petals. Unlike dry pot pourri, the petals for moist pot pourri must not be left to dry out completely: they should be partially dry with a rather limp, leathery feel to them. Prepare the petals when they are freshly picked and their fragrance is at its most pungent. Place them on a tray, one layer deep, in a cool, dry, well-ventilated place, preferably in the dark (under the bed is perfect); large petals should take only three or four days to be ready, tiny petals take two or three days. Check their progress daily so that you catch them just at the right moment.

You will then begin to layer the petals and salt in the straight-sided pot. You will need a fair quantity of petals – normally about 4lb (2kg) of petals to 1lb (500gm) salt. If you do not have this quantity of petals available at once, you can add them in the following days, until you have built up to the required amount.

When the layering is complete, place a plate that will fit snuggly into the crock on top of the mixture and put a very heavy weight on top of the plate to press the contents down. Stir the contents daily for between 10 and 14 days, so if you intend adding more petals, these should be added last in layers with the salt, then pressed down as before with the plate and weight. During this fermenting time, you may notice

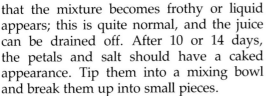

that the mixture becomes frothy or liquid appears; this is quite normal, and the juice can be drained off. After 10 or 14 days, the petals and salt should have a caked appearance. Tip them into a mixing bowl and break them up into small pieces.

The next step is to add the other dried ingredients, such as herbs, spices and oils, and other completely dried flower petals, such as lavender or different types of rose. Mix your chosen fragrances together extremely well and return them to the crock. Press the ingredients down once again, using the plate and weight, and cover the crock with some fine fabric such as gauze or muslin, which should be secured around the rim. Then put the crock in a well-ventilated, cool, dark place such as a pantry or larder for a further six weeks.

ROSE PETAL MOIST POT POURRI

This is an adaptation of several old recipes and will make enough pot pourri to fill a good sized bowl. If you do not have the types of roses listed below, simply use the strongest scented types you have.

YOU WILL NEED

4lb 8oz (2kg) rose petals, preferably as a mix of: 2lb 4oz (1kg) damask rose petals; 2lb 4oz (1kg) moss rose petals

2oz (60gm) rose geranium leaves

4oz (125gm) lavender florets

4oz (125gm) rose buds

2oz (60gm) lemon verbena leaves

2oz (60gm) orris-root powder

1lb (500gm) rock salt (non-iodized)

½oz (15gm) ground cinnamon

½oz (15gm) ground nutmeg

4 drops rose geranium oil

2 drops tea rose oil

2 drops damask rose oil

2 drops lavender oil

1 measure of brandy

Finely grated rind of 2 lemons

Place the semi-dry leathery rose petals in layers about 1/2in (12mm) deep, with the grated lemon rind, orris-root powder and salt. Cover with a plate and weight and leave to cure for about 10 days, stirring daily or until the mixture has caked. Place the mixture in a mixing bowl and pull it into small pieces. Then add all the other dried ingredients, the herbs, spices, fixatives, oils and the brandy, and mix them thoroughly with a wooden spoon. Return to the crock, cover once again with the plate and weight, and cover with muslin before leaving to cure for six weeks. If you do not wish to use the pot pourri immediately, store in a tightly sealed jar.

DRY POT POURRI

Apart from the wonderful range of fragrances, colour is a vital factor in making any pot pourri. There are such an overwhelming number of flowers to choose from and so many different combinations to place together, that trying to make a decision becomes a major task!

The first point to consider is the decoration of the room in which you wish to place the pot pourri. You may have chosen a container that is a particular tint, which will then have to be matched to the flowers and other ingredients. If you have no preconceived ideas, consider the surroundings carefully and decide where the container will be placed and how large you want it to be. Then decide which type of colouring will be best for the room. If, for example, your living-room is decorated in pastel shades, with the emphasis on soft, warm colours, pinks, golds, greens and creams will usually match beautifully. If the room is decorated in cooler tints, such as lilacs, greys or blues, there are the most wonderful shades of larkspurs, lavender and cornflowers to suit the mood. The fragrance can be decided when you have chosen the colour of the flowers, although, obviously, if you wish to display only rose petals or buds, the fragrance will already have been decided for you. You can still alter the scent, however, by adding other ingredients that will either blend with or override the existing perfumes.

Some fragrances are better suited to some rooms than to others, but ultimately, of course, the choice will depend on your own taste. Living areas where you may entertain guests often benefit from having a warm and welcoming perfume that is not too overpowering but is the scent of just one

OVERLEAF: ingredients for pot pourri (page 132): fir cones, blade mace, cotton pods, uva-ursi leaves, bakuli pods, marigold flowers, calamus (sweet sedge) root, red sandalwood, bay leaves, sunflower petals, hibiscus pods and achillea; (page 133) blue malva, cornflowers, bougainvillaea, black mallow, red rose buds, lavender florets, pale pink rose petals, achillea 'The Pearl', bene flowers, hibiscus flowers, rose buds, mauve larkspur, pink larkspur, statice flowers and rose petals.

flower. Pot pourri can be too strong, just as one can use too much perfume on oneself. The scent should be there, fragrancing the room without overpowering it. Blends that have been made using citric fruit, cinnamon and other fairly spicy scents usually suit both men's and women's tastes, and they are also suitable for kitchens and dining areas. Lavender and rose mixes are popular for virtually any reception room, while roses are probably the most popular blends for bedrooms.

Pot pourri benefits from being placed in a warm room so that the fragrances are drawn out naturally. Placing the container under the warmth of a table lamp or on a table near a radiator will benefit permeation. If the room is very large, it is often better to divide a larger quantity into two smaller bowls that can be placed in different parts of the room.

On the pages that follow five mixes of pot pourri are given – there is one for each season and a special Christmas blend. Some of the ingredients may not be available from your garden, and many of the different herbs, spices, fixatives and oils will have to be bought from a specialist store (see page 156). Before you begin, however, make sure that you have the accessories listed below.

SPRING POT POURRI

These ingredients will fill a big bowl and would be ideal for a large bedroom or even a living room. The bowl I used was very large; if you wish to make a smaller amount, halve the quantities listed below. The pastel colours are delightfully delicate and will remind you of the mass of flowers that begin to appear during spring.

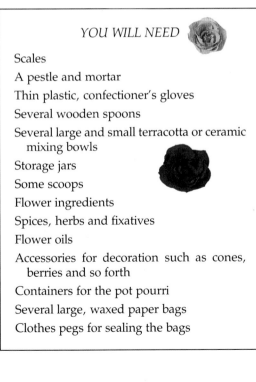

YOU WILL NEED

Scales

A pestle and mortar

Thin plastic, confectioner's gloves

Several wooden spoons

Several large and small terracotta or ceramic mixing bowls

Storage jars

Some scoops

Flower ingredients

Spices, herbs and fixatives

Flower oils

Accessories for decoration such as cones, berries and so forth

Containers for the pot pourri

Several large, waxed paper bags

Clothes pegs for sealing the bags

YOU WILL NEED

Flowers

1lb (500gm) pink rose buds

1lb 4oz (600gm) bougainvillaea flowers

6oz (180gm) sunflower petals

6oz (180gm) chamomile heads

2oz (60gm) cotton lavender

4oz (125gm) pink rose petals

6oz (180gm) cream rose petals

8oz (250gm) lavender florets

Flowers for decorating the surface

A handful of whole peony leaves

A handful of golden rod florets (caught when green)

20 deep blue, whole lavender heads

A handful of hydrangea flowers

6-8 whole yellow rose heads

A handful of deep pink peony petals

6-8 lantana seed pods

Spices and fixatives

4oz (125gm) ground orris-root powder

1oz (30gm) allspice

2oz (60gm) ground cinnamon

1oz (30gm) ground cloves

2oz (60gm) ground dried lemon peel

Essential oils

4 drops lemon verbena

8 drops rose oil

1 drop patchouili oil

2 drops lavender oil

OPPOSITE: preparing to make pot pourri.

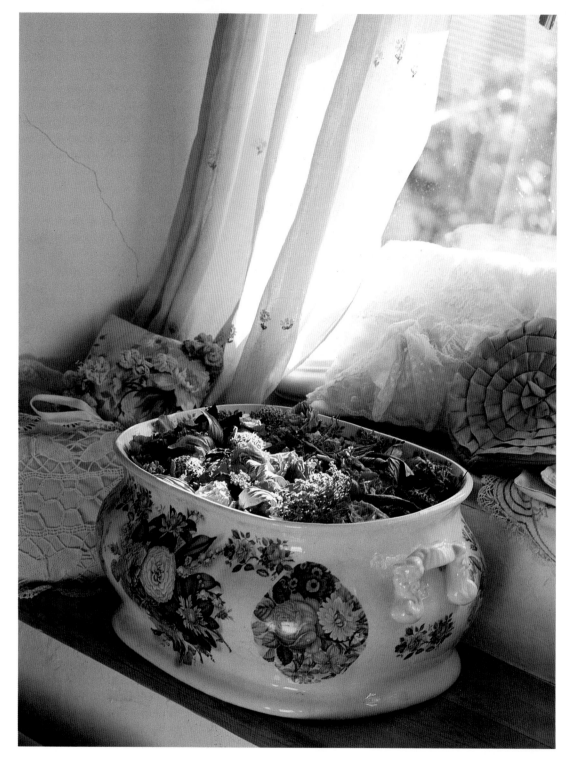

Spring pot pourri.

Combine all the flower ingredients in a large mixing bowl and place all the herbs, spices and fixatives in another, smaller bowl and mix well, using a wooden spoon. When I mix the flower petals, I find it better to use my hands rather than a spoon, which can easily damage the fragile petals. (Very thin confectioner's or medical gloves, which can usually be bought at a chemists, are perfect for this.) Carefully add the herbs, spices and fixatives to the flowers, making sure that there are no lumps. Add the essential oils last of all, taking care not to overdo it! Place all the ingredients in a large waxed paper bag and seal it tightly. Stir the contents gently every other day, then seal the bag again. This mixture should be left to mellow for two to three weeks.

SUMMER POT POURRI

This is the simplest pot pourri to make; it requires few ingredients but produces the prettiest effect. The blend is wonderful for a bedroom, where the smell will linger when the room is not in use. The quantities are enough for a small to medium sized bowl.

YOU WILL NEED

Flowers

8-10oz (250-300gm) tiny pink rose buds

3 large pink peony heads for decoration

Fixatives

2oz (60gm) orris-root powder

Oils

2 drops damask rose oil

2 drops rose geranium oil

2 drops lemon verbena oil

Place the rose buds in a mixing bowl and add the orris-root, turning the buds while you do this. Cover the bowl with a plate and leave it for 48 hours, turning the mixture a couple of times during the two days. Add the drops of each of the oils in turn, mixing well all the time, and then place the mixture in a waxed paper bag and leave it sealed for two weeks. Turn the contents every other day, resealing each time. When the mixture is ready, pour it into a pretty bowl and decorate it with the peony heads.

Summer pot pourri.

AUTUMN POT POURRI

Many people adore autumn with its changing colours and fresher days, but I find it rather melancholy, and it is the time of year when I search for ideas to brighten up my home. This pot pourri is warm and vibrant in colour, and I love glancing at it on my kitchen shelf. The fragrance is delightfully spicy, and the ingredients are simple and attractive. These quantities will be sufficient for a medium sized bowl.

YOU WILL NEED

Flowers

6oz (180gm) whole marigold heads

2oz (60gm) yellow achillea flowers

4oz (125gm) uva-ursi (bearberry) leaves

2oz (60gm) hibiscus pods

1oz (30gm) cotton pods

1oz (30gm) small fir cones

1oz (30gm) bakuli heads

3oz (90gm) broom flowers

4-6 orange or peach whole rose heads

Herbs and spices

2oz (60gm) whole blade mace

3oz (90gm) whole cinnamon sticks

2oz (60gm) whole star anise heads

2oz (60gm) tiny red chillies

1oz (30gm) ground cinnamon

1oz (30gm) ground cloves

1oz (30gm) ground allspice

3oz (90gm) orris-root powder

1oz (30gm) small pieces of sandalwood

2oz (60gm) ground dried orange peel

Oils

1 drop cedarwood oil

2 drops sandalwood oil

1 drop patchouli oil

2 drops orange flower oil

Before mixing the ingredients together, you should break the achillea heads into florets and cut the cinnamon sticks into small lengths. Using 5½oz (165gm) of the marigold flowers, mix all the flower ingredients together in a large bowl. In a separate, smaller bowl, blend together all the herbs, spices and fixatives, pressing out any lumps that may be present. When they are thor-

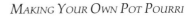

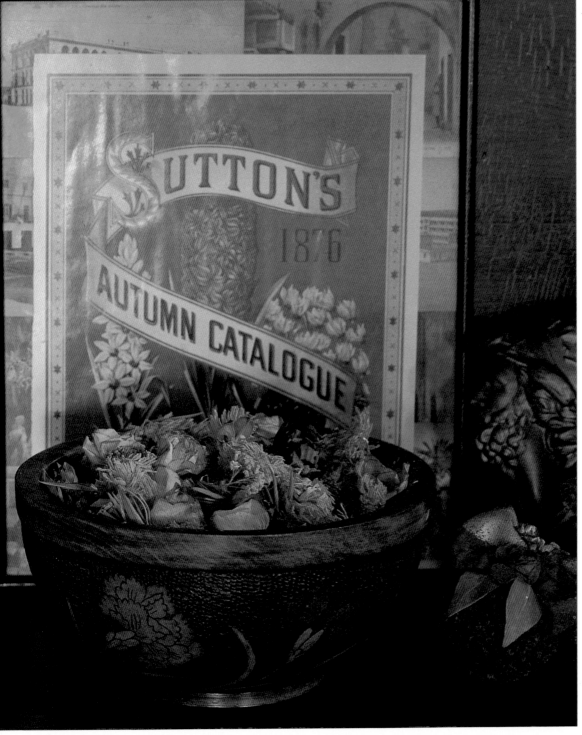

Autumn pot pourri.

oughly mixed, pour the contents into the flower ingredients. Place the whole mixture in a waxed paper bag, seal it and leave for one week, turning the contents frequently during this time.

The next step is to add the oils. Return the contents to a large mixing bowl and add the drops carefully, mixing all the time. This mixture should then be replaced in the paper

bag and left for a further three weeks. When the recipe is ready, place it in a container.

This mixture looks particularly attractive in wooden or terracotta bowls. Place the last ½oz (15gm) of marigold heads on top of the bowl, and extract several cones, pods, achillea florets and cinnamon sticks. When these are placed around the marigold heads, the pot pourri will look simply stunning.

Winter pot pourri.

WINTER POT POURRI

I love this brilliantly coloured winter mixture. Although blue is often considered a cold colour, mixed with crimson rose petals, as here, it cannot fail to brighten any room, and the blend of lavender, rose, lemon and eucalyptus is exquisitely fresh and a wonderful perfume if you are suffering from a cold!

YOU WILL NEED

Flowers

6oz (180gm) vivid blue cornflower heads

6oz (180gm) lavender florets

4oz (125gm) blue mallow flowers

2oz (60gm) blue larkspur florets

2oz (60gm) lilac coloured statice florets

2oz (60gm) black mallow heads

3oz (90gm) deep crimson rose petals

3 whole, large, crimson rose heads for surface decoration

Herbs, spices and fixatives

2oz (60gm) orris-root powder

1oz (30gm) ground cinnamon

1oz (30gm) dried mint

Oils

6 drops lavender oil

2 drops lemon verbena oil

1 drop rose geranium oil

2 drops eucalyptus oil

Mix all the flower ingredients together in a large bowl, leaving the rose heads on one side for decoration. Mix the herbs, spices and fixatives together in a small bowl, and then add this mixture to the flowers. Take each oil in turn, carefully blending the drops with the mixture. Place all the ingredients in a waxed paper bag, seal it and leave for two weeks. Turn the contents of the bag every two days. When the mixture is ready, place the contents in a bowl and arrange a mixture of the cornflower heads, rose petals and the whole rose heads on the surface. Because it is so incredibly blue, this mixture looks wonderful in a container to match, and Spode china is particularly attractive filled with this recipe.

CHRISTMAS POT POURRI

This is the most festive-looking blend. Made with traditional Christmas colours, it is the perfect centre-piece for a sideboard decoration in the dining-room, or, if you place the container on a low table near a blazing log fire, the warmth will draw out the fragrances, and the room will be filled with the traditional scents of spicy herbs. The ingredients below will fill a large bowl.

YOU WILL NEED

Flowers

8oz (250gm) crimson rose petals

2oz (60gm) achillea 'The Pearl' florets

2oz (60gm) bene flowers

3oz (90gm) hibiscus flowers

1oz (30gm) bakuli heads

3oz (90gm) small fir cones

2oz (60gm) small, deep pink rose heads

For decoration

Whole peppercorn stems

Whole, deep red rose heads

6-8 wooden rose heads

Herbs

2oz (60gm) cardamom pods

1oz (30gm) whole bay leaves

3oz (90gm) rosemary

2oz (60gm) chamomile flowers

Spices and fixatives

2oz (60gm) orris-root powder

1oz (30gm) powdered cinnamon

1oz (30gm) allspice

½oz (15gm) ground cloves

½oz (15gm) ground nutmeg

½oz (15gm) ground orange rind

½oz (15gm) ground lemon rind

Oils

1 drop bergamot oil

1 drop lemon verbena oil

This mixture will take three or four weeks to make, so if you are planning to make pot pourri for Christmas, you will need to start in November. Place all the flower ingredients together in a large bowl and mix carefully. In a smaller bowl, mix together all the herbs, spices and fixatives. Add the contents of this bowl to the flowers and mix thoroughly. Place all the mixture in a large, waxed paper bag and seal it. Turn the mixture every other day for 10 days, then leave it to cure for a further five days without disturbing it. Then place all the contents again in a large mixing bowl and add the oils. Return the contents to the bag and leave it sealed for a further 10-15 days. When the blend is ready, tip it into a large container, arranging the cones, peppercorns and wooden rose heads on the surface, together with several large deep red or deep pink rose heads if you feel you want to add more.

When you make your own pot pourri, you may find that you prefer to emphasize one fragrance rather than another, so I suggest that before you begin you should try smelling all the essential oils that are mentioned. If you do not like one, either replace it with another or leave it out altogether, altering the recipe to suit your own taste. For example, if you do not like the fragrance of damask rose oil, but adore tea rose, just use tea rose.

OPPOSITE: Christmas pot pourri.

OTHER SCENTED IDEAS

A basket decorated around the rim with pink peonies, lupidium, lavender, silene, roses, hydrangeas, oregano and curry plant. Such a basket is ideal for displaying pot pourri.

There are numerous items and articles that can be created using flowers and herbs that have a strong fragrance. Many of these date back to the time of our great-grand-mothers and even earlier, but they are still as popular today as then. Some of these items can be made quite easily, and they are perfect for fragrancing your home or for making as charming presents for a special occasion.

DECORATED POT POURRI BASKET

This is a particularly attractive way of displaying your pot pourri, and it can be made either very simply or very elaborately, depending on the effect you wish to achieve. The method is the same for both versions, but the elaborate type (illustrated above) will require far more flowers and will take longer

to make. To make the basket, work around the brim to create a type of swag, wiring the little bunches on to the weave. Choose a basket with a strong, fairly coarse weave so that you can push the wires through without difficulty.

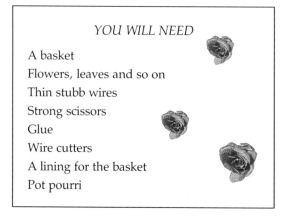

YOU WILL NEED

A basket

Flowers, leaves and so on

Thin stubb wires

Strong scissors

Glue

Wire cutters

A lining for the basket

Pot pourri

You will need a large, clear work space to make this basket. You can either use small bunches of mixed flowers or bunches of all one type, but whichever you choose, begin by making as many bunches as possible so that you do not have to keep stopping. Select the bunches you wish to use, and, taking each type in turn, cut the stems to the length required. The bunches will then be wired to the brim using the stubb wires. There are two ways of doing this. If you simply wish to make a single row around the brim, wire the first bunch to the basket, then attach the second, overlapping the stems of the first. This will create a fairly simple, but quite dainty effect, and it is particularly suitable for baskets with narrow rims. The other method is to place the bunches at different angles; for example, you would wire one facing out, the next angled towards the inside and so on until the rim is filled. If your basket has a handle, begin work next to the handle, with the flower tips pressed as closely to it as possible to avoid unnecessary gaps. When you have worked around the rim and get to the handle on the other side, reverse the last little bunch to hide the stems. If you find this difficult, you could try placing one larger flower here instead, and, to balance the overall effect, another of the

same type of flower at your starting point, wiring the flowers over the first bunch.

When the basket is ready, line the inside with non-absorbent paper or foil before placing the pot pourri inside; this will prevent little pieces falling through the weave or a ring being left on wooden surfaces. If the basket is to be a gift, especially a wedding gift, bind the handle with satin ribbon.

POMANDERS

Pomanders have been used for centuries, but not necessarily in the form with which we are familiar today. The word pomander derives from the French *pomme d'ambre*, which was a round piece of ambergris, a highly scented fixative. The ambergris was placed in a beautiful hollow ball made of gold, silver, ivory or wood, which was normally worn suspended from the belt by a small chain, to ward off the evil smells that filled the street – and those emanating from other people! Today, pomanders are usually made from china balls, perforated with small holes that allow the contents of sweet-smelling pot pourri or herbs to permeate their fragrance into the area in which they are placed.

The ingredients for making a pomander from citrus fruits and cloves: oranges, ground spices (including cinnamon, orris-root, whole cloves and a mixture of allspice and nutmeg) and essential oils (bergamot, cinnamon and clove). Also shown are an orange that has been taped ready for use, a knitting needle, a fork, tape, scissors and a box of large-headed pins.

Finished and cured pomanders, decorated with festive ribbons.

There are two other types of pomander, which are not only attractive but are easy to make and very effective. The first is a pomander made from citrus fruit pierced with cloves and left to cure in a number of spices. These are traditionally regarded as Christmas pomanders, but I have a large bowl filled with them in my dining-room and it gives the most wonderful fragrance all through the year. Making pomanders like this is something that children enjoy doing enormously, and with many pairs of willing hands to help you will have them made in no time!

Although these pomanders can be made from any citrus fruit, I think my favourites are those made with oranges. Choose small oranges if possible – they require less filling and are more economical on ribbon. The ribbons can be any type and colour, but I think they look particularly attractive using either tartan or velvet ribbon.

The recipe below is for two orange pomanders. If you wish to make a larger quantity, say six pomanders, double the quantities. The fragrance of your finished pomander, will last for years, although they do shrink in size. If you need to revive the fragrance, run the pomander under warm water, remove excess water and replace it in the curing mixture for several weeks, and it will smell as wonderful as ever. These pomanders will bring fresh, new fragrance to drawers, wardrobes or any enclosed space.

Unless your working surface is Formica or some similar material, I suggest that you put down newspaper before you begin. Place the ribbon tape around the orange, keeping it as even as possible; if you wish, you can place a second tape around the orange to create four different sections. Place pins 2in (5cm) apart in each side of the tape so that it does not slip out of position. When you have finished inserting the cloves, you will remove the tape, leaving channels for the ribbon.

Pierce the surface of the orange with the knitting needle; cloves tend to be rather hard to push in by themselves and sometimes break with the pressure. After the initial hole, it is often quicker to use a four-pronged fork, which will leave the correct spaces between each clove. Complete the first circuit, working close to the tape, which you should use as a guide line, then add a second row, leaving a small gap between the

Two rose bud pomanders, decorated with ribbons and ready for use, and, on the right, a foam ball showing how the rose buds should be positioned.

rows. Continue until both oranges are evenly covered. When you are satisfied with the results, mix the spices in a bowl, eliminating any lumps, add the drops of oil and, having removed the tape, place the pomanders in this mixture, turn them, and, using a wooden spoon, place some of the powder on top of them. Cover the bowl with muslin and place it in a warm, dry place. Turn the pomanders every day; they sometimes take up to six weeks to be completely cured, so if you are planning to use them at Christmas-time, you will have to make a start in early November.

To decorate the pomanders, gently brush off any excess powder – a very soft toothbrush is good for this purpose – and bind the ribbon around the channels. Tie a knot and make a bow. If you wish to suspend them, place some ribbon through the top, tying it securely to the first pieces, and then another knot at the ribbon ends.

ROSE BUD POMANDERS

This type of pomander can be made using virtually any type of dried flower, but I think rose bud pomanders are the prettiest. The buds usually have convenient little stalks to place into the sphere, and it is possible to find shops that will sell the scented rose buds in the form of pot pourri. If you cannot obtain the buds, you can prepare them in the same way as for the Summer Pot Pourri (see page 137). The spheres will smell wonderful and can be hung or placed in wardrobes, drawers or linen cupboards, or suspended in a room, such as on a dressing-table mirror or from a bed post. They look simply beautiful when decorated with matching satin ribbon and make the most delightful gift, looking particularly pretty when placed in a delicately designed box filled with pastel tissue paper.

YOU WILL NEED

A small plastic foam (Oasis) sphere

4-6oz (125-180gm) scented rose buds

Several medium gauge stubb wires, 6in (15cm) long

Wire cutters

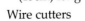

Scissors

12in (30cm) medium width satin ribbon for the bow

36in (90cm) narrow satin ribbon for suspending and decorating

Glue

If you intend to hang up the sphere, you will first have to place wire through the foam ball. To do this, take one wire and bend it in half. Push the pointed ends right through the middle of the ball, keeping them parallel. When the wires appear, pull them through so that the loop end rests on the ball. Bend each wire back, away from the other, and up, towards the ball. Pull the loop back up so that there is enough space for the ribbons. This will secure the wire for suspending, and it is wise to use a thread to mark the loop so that you do not lose it as you work!

Working with one rose bud at a time, begin near the loop, placing the rose buds in a straight line round to the other side of the sphere and back up to meet the loop again. Place the rose buds as close together as possible, and each row as close as possible to the next to hide the foam. If a stalk snaps during insertion, glue the rose bud to the foam.

When you have covered the sphere, take the narrow ribbon and cut off 12in (30cm). Fold it in half and tie it to the wire loop with a knot. Tie another knot where the ribbon ends meet, and cut the ends diagonally to prevent their fraying. Then fold the medium width ribbon in half and make a bow through the wire. The rest of the narrow ribbon will be suspended from underneath the sphere. Cut it into three lengths and tie them with a knot. Cut a stubb wire to 3in (7.5cm) long, bend it in half and push it over the ribbons and firmly into the foam ball (see the illustration on page 147). The sphere is now ready to place in position. If you find that the fragrance fades in time, revive it using tiny drops of rose oil.

LAVENDER BOTTLES

Lavender is the most delightful of flowers, and no garden should be without a bush of this fragrant and versatile plant. Picked fresh, it is wonderful for using in fresh-flower arrangements; dried, it can be used whole in displays or, shedded, it can be made into pot pourri or used to fragrance sachets and pillows. Lavender oil has potent healing properties and is widely used in aromatherapy, as well as being the base for many modern perfumes, soaps and other beauty products.

When I was little, I used to wonder what created the evocative scent in our airing cupboard. When I grew tall enough to see the upper shelves, I discovered some fragrant, ribboned sticks, which, I was told, were lavender bottles. I have never been without them during all my adult life, and they are a most charming idea to pass down to one's children and a perfect occupation for a rainy afternoon. The idea dates back at least to our great-grandmothers and possibly in different forms even earlier, but it is something that I feel sure will continue for ever.

Use one of the taller growing varieties to make your lavender bottles. Although 'Hidcote' is possibly the most fragrant variety, it is rather short and fiddly to use.

YOU WILL NEED

40-50 stems of lavender, 18-20in (45-50cm) long

Raffia or thin string

36-48in (0.9-1.2m) narrow satin ribbon

12in (30cm) medium satin ribbon for the bow

Strong scissors

A blunt-ended ribbon-theading needle

Sort the stems into even lengths, keeping all the heads together, and remove any roots or excess leaves from the stems. Using the raffia or string, tie a tight knot just under the heads to form a bunch. Holding the heads, pull each stalk back over them to form a cage, keeping the little florets inside the stems (see the illustration on page 150). When you have worked around the heads, take the raffia or string and tie it tightly around the base of the cage (see the illustration on page 150). Trim the ends of the stems and remove any leaves that are sticking out.

Thread the needle with the ribbon, pulling just over half the ribbon through the eye, and, beginning at the top of the bottle, pull all the ribbon through except for 4in (10cm), which you will tie into a knot around the first stem and then feed into your work when you have finished. Begin threading the ribbon over and under the stems, jumping three or four stems at a time and pulling the ribbon as tight as possible because the stems shrink when they dry. When you have completed the first circuit, you alternate by

OPPOSITE: rows of lavender drying in a shed.

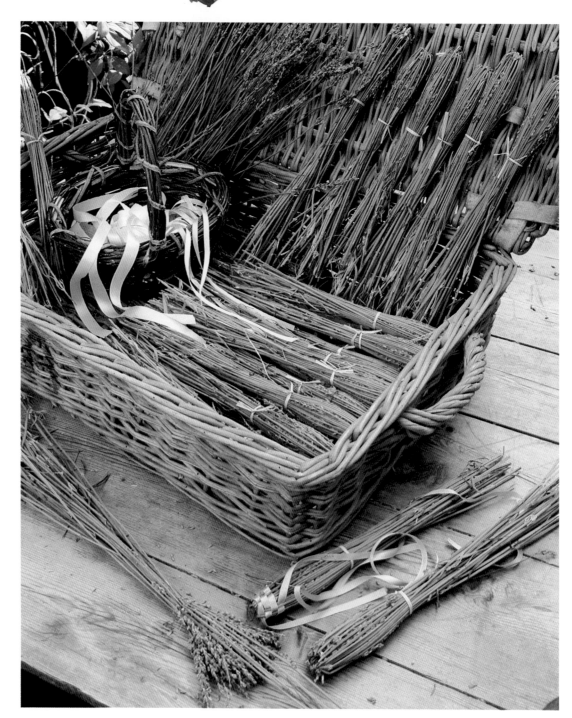

The three stages of making lavender bottles: first, the lavender is bunched, second, the stems are bent over to form a cage, and finally, the bunch is ready for the ribbon to be woven through the stems.

OPPOSITE: the finished lavender bottles are prettily decorated with pastel-coloured ribbons.

going over or under the stem next to the first stem to create a basket effect. This does require practice, so do not loose heart. You may find it difficult to begin with, but by the time you are half-way down, it becomes far simpler! When you get to the raffia or string, wind the ribbon several times round the stalks and tie a tight knot.

Turn the stick so that the ribboned end faces you and, using the remaining ribbon folded in half, tie a knot at the stem end, about 2in (5cm) up. Criss-cross the ribbon up the stems, and when you get to the heads, wind the ribbon round and tie another tight knot to finish off. Take the wider piece of ribbon and tie it round the base below the cage to cover the point where you finished off the narrow ribbons and knots.

The bottles should now be left to dry, which will take about two weeks. Place them on a tray, leaving a space between each, and leave them in a warm, dry place out of direct light. When they are dry, they can be placed in a drawer or cupboard.

Pillows and sachets filled with fragrant pot pourri.

SCENTED SACHETS AND PILLOWS

It is said that the fragrance of hops will send you into the most glorious sleep. I have never had problems sleeping, so I cannot pretend to give you this information first hand! I do know, however, that the gentle fragrance of herbs and flowers near the bedside gives great comfort and a feeling of well-being. Sachets and pillows are easy to make, and you do not have to be an expert at needlework. I buy pretty pillow slips and fabric cases at antique shops and on market stalls, make a lining to go inside them and then fill them with the fragrance of my choice. Some perfumes are too overpowering to have permanently near you, so I always choose a delicate herbal scent or softly fragranced flowers to fill the bags. Herbs such as lemon balm, mint, rosemary and sweet marjoram are all great favourites, and they can be used on their own or mixed

with other scents. Lavender is wonderful on its own, and its perfume will last for years. Below are some simple mixes to try, and when you tire of one, just remove the sachet and make another.

There are two types of sachets. The first type are seen in drawers and on shelves, while the second is used for fragrancing a pillow and is not visible. To make the first type, you will want to choose a pretty fabric. Antique shops and market stalls as well as traditional material stores often have beautiful remnants for sale. Avoid materials with huge designs, which will be lost on these small sachets. Instead, choose pretty little flower designs, small stripes, check or even completely plain fabrics. Natural materials – cottons, silks and satins – are the nicest, and if you choose lace, you will probably have to line the inside with a fine, plain fabric or the pot pourri will fall through the holes.

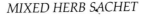

A SACHET FOR DRAWERS OR SHELVES

YOU WILL NEED

A rectangular piece of fabric, 12 x 8in
 (30 x 20cm)

A needle and thread

Sewing scissors

12-18in (30-45cm) ribbon

Pot pourri

An iron

Turn the fabric inside out and fold it in half. Sew neatly up both the open sides, then fold the top of the bag about one-third of the way down and iron it flat. Place a stitch on each side so that the fabric will not slip back out. Turn the bag the right way out and fill it about two-thirds full of the pot pourri. Take the ribbon, wind it around twice, tie a tight knot and then make a bow. The sachet is now ready to use.

AN INTERIOR SACHET

YOU WILL NEED

A rectangular piece of plain fabric, 12 x 18in
 (30 x 20cm)

Sewing scissors

A needle and thread

Pot pourri

An iron

Turn the fabric inside out and fold it in half. Sew neatly up both the open sides, then turn the top of the bag back about 1in (2.5cm) down and iron flat. Catch each side with a piece of thread and turn the bag the right way out. Fill the bag with the pot pourri and sew the top neatly together. Before leaving it inside a pillowcase, remove the pillow and sew two corners of the bag to the pillow to prevent it slipping. Do not make tight knots or it will be difficult to remove later on. Replace the pillow in the slip, and the sachet will almost immediately begin to fragrance the pillow.

SLEEP PILLOW

This quantity will be sufficient
 to fill three sachets

1oz (30gm) hops

1oz (30gm) rosemary

1oz (30gm) lemon verbena leaves

1 drop lemon verbena oil

LAVENDER SACHET

This quantity will be
 sufficient to fill two sachets

3oz (90gm) lavender florets

1oz (30gm) peppermint leaves

2 drops lavender oil

MIXED HERB SACHET

This quantity will fill four sachets

1oz (30gm) peppermint leaves

1oz (30gm) rosemary

1oz (30gm) thyme

1oz (30gm) lemon verbena

1oz (30gm) sweet woodruff

1oz (30gm) Chamomile flowers

1 drop lemon balm oil

ROSE SACHET

This quantity will fill three
 sachets

4oz (125gm) rose petals

1oz (30gm) whole rose buds

½oz (15gm) whole cloves

½oz (15gm) orris-root powder

2 drops damask rose oil

There are many combinations of herbs and flowers that are delightful when mixed together, and, as each person will prefer a different type of fragrance, experiment with herbs and flowers from your garden to produce wonderful results. Remember not to add too many drops of oil as the effect will be overpowering.

PROTECTED WILD PLANTS

These plants are specially protected
in Britain by the Wildlife and Countryside Act
1981. It is an offence to pick, remove
or sell them.

Adder's tongue spearwort *Ranunculus ophioglossifolius*
Alpine catchfly *Lychnis alpina*
Alpine gentian *Gentiana nivalis*
Alpine sow-thistle *Cicerbita alpina*
Alpine woodsia *Woodsia alpina*
Bedstraw broomrape *Orobanche caryophyllacea*
Blue heath *Phyllodoce caerulea*
Brown galingale *Gyperus fuscus*
Cheddar pink *Dianthus gratianopolitanus*
Childling pink *Petrorhagia nanteuilii*
Diapensia *Diapensia lapponica*
Dickie's bladder-fern *Cystopteris dickieana*
Downy woundwort *Stachys germanica*
Drooping saxifrage *Saxifraga cernua*
Early spider-orchid *Ophrys sphegodes*
Fen orchid *Liparis loeselii*
Fen violet *Viola persicifolia*
Field cow-wheat *Melampyrum arvense*
Field eryngo *Eryngium campestre*
Field wormwood *Artemisia campestris*
Ghost orchid *Epipogium aphyllum*
Greater yellow-rattle *Rhinanthus serotinus*
Jersey cudweed *Gnaphalium luteoalbum*
Killarney fern *Trichomanes speciosum*
Lady's-slipper *Cypripedium calceolus*
Late spider-orchid *Ophrys fuciflora*
Least lettuce *Lactuca saligna*
Limestone woundwort *Stachys alpina*
Lizard orchid *Himantoglossum hircinum*
Military orchid *Orchis militaris*
Monkey orchid *Orchis simia*

Norwegian sandwort *Arenaria norvegica*
Oblong woodsia *Woodsia ilvensis*
Oxtongue broomrape *Orobanche loricata*
Perennial knawel *Scleranthus perennis*
Plymouth pear *Pyrus cordata*
Purple spurge *Euphorbia peplis*
Red helleborine *Cephalanthera rubra*
Ribbon-leaved water-plantain *Alisma gramineum*
Rock cinquefoil *Potentilla rupestris*
Rock sea-lavender (two rare species) *Limonium paradoxum/Limonium recurvum*
Rough marsh-mallow *Althaea hirsuta*
Round-headed leek *Allium sphaerocephalon*
Sea knotgrass *Polygonum maritimum*
Sickle-leaved hare's-ear *Bupleurum falcatum*
Small alison *Alyssum alyssoides*
Small hare's-ear *Bupleurum baldense*
Snowdon lily *Lloydia serotina*
Spiked speedwell *Veronica spicata*
Spring gentian *Gentiana verna*
Starfruit *Damasonium alisma*
Starved wood-sedge *Carex depauperata*
Teesdale sandwort *Minuartia stricta*
Thistle broomrape *Orobanche reticulata*
Triangular club-rush *Scirpus triquetrus*
Tufted saxifrage *Saxifraga cespitosa*
Water germander *Teucrium scordium*
Whorled solomon's-seal *Polygonatum verticillatum*
Wild cotoneaster *Cotoneaster integerrimus*
Wild gladiolus *Gladiolus illyricus*
Wood calamint *Calamintha sylvatica*

For readers in the United States and Canada
Always make sure the plant is not
considered rare or endangered before you
pick it. US readers please check with your
state Natural Heritage Program or similar
state agency for a list of endangered species;
Canadian readers should check with the
proper provincial authority.

THE LANGUAGE OF FLOWERS

Acacia – chaste love
Acanthus – the fine arts, artifice
Achillea millefolium – war
Aconite (wolfsbane) – misanthropy
Aconite (crowfoot) – lustre
Agrimony – thankfulness, gratitude
Allspice – compassion
Amaranth – immortality, unfading love
Amaranth, cockscomb – foppery, affectation
Anemone, field – sickness
Anemone, garden – forsaken
Angelica – inspiration
Apple blossom – preference
Ash, mountain – prudence
Asparagus fern – secrecy
Aster, double – reciprocity

Bachelor's buttons – single blessedness
Banksia – love sweet and silent
Basil – hatred
Bay – glory
Beech tree – prosperity
Bellflower, white – gratitude
Bindweed, greater – insinuation
Bindweed, lesser – humility
Birch – meekness
Black poplar – courage
Bluebell – constancy
Borage – bluntness
Box – firmness
Bramble – lowliness, envy, remorse
Broom – humility
Buttercup – childhood

Campanula – you are rich in attraction
Chamomile – energy in adversity
Carnation – woman's love
Celandine – joy
Chestnut – do me justice
Chrysanthemum – cheerfulness
Clematis – poverty
Cloves – dignity
Clover, four-leaved – be mine
Colt's-foot – justice shall be done
Columbine – resolution
Convolvulus – bonds, uncertainty
Coriander – concealed merit
Corn – riches
Corn cockle – duration
Cowslip – pensiveness
Crocus – abuse not
Cypress – mourning

Daffodil – regard
Daisy, garden – I share your sentiment
Daisy, ox-eye – a token
Dandelion – oracle
Daphne – ornament
Dock – patience
Dogwood – durability

Elder – zealousness
Elm – dignity
Escallonia – I live for thee
Eucalyptus – farewell
Evening primrose – inconstancy
Everlasting pea – wilt thou go with me?

Fennel – worthy of all praise
Fern – sincerity
Fir – elevation
Fir cone – order

Flax – domestic virtues
Fleur-de-lys – flame
Fool's parsley – silliness
Foxglove – insincerity
French marigold – jealousy
Fuchsia – taste

Gardenia – peace
Geranium, pink – partiality
Geranium, scarlet – comfort
Gilliflower – lasting beauty
Golden rod – precaution, encouragement
Gorse – enduring affection
Grass – utility

Harebell – grief
Hawthorn – hope
Hazel – reconciliation
Heartsease or *pansy* – you occupy my thoughts
Hellebore – scandal, calumny
Hemlock – you will be my death
Hibiscus – change
Hogweed – remembrance
Holly – forethought
Hollyhock – female ambition
Honesty – fascination
Honeysuckle – rustic beauty
Hop – injustice
Houseleek – vivacity
Hyacinth – sport, game, play
Hydrangea – boastfulness
Hyssop – purity

Indian pink – always lovely
Iris – I have a message for you
Ivy – friendship

Japonica – love at first sight
Jasmine, white – extreme amiability
Jasmine, yellow – grace and elegance
Juniper – protection

Kalmia – nature
Kingcup – I wish I was rich
Knotweed – recantation

Laburnum – forsaken
Lady's slipper – capricious beauty
Lantana – rigour
Larch – audacity
Larkspur – brightness
Laurel – ambition
Lavender – distrust
Lemon – piquancy
Lilac – first emotions of love
Lily-of-the-valley – return of happiness
Love-lies-bleeding – hopeless

Magnolia – love of nature
Marjoram – blushes
Marshmallow – kindness
Meadow saffron – mirth
Meadowsweet – uselessness
Mignonette – excellence
Mint – virtue
Mistletoe – I surmount all obstacles
Monkshood – fickleness
Moss – seclusion
Mountain ash – intellect
Myrtle – love

Narcissus – egotism

Nasturtium – patriotism
Nettle, common stinging – you are cruel
Night-scented stock – devotion

Oak – hospitality
Oats – music
Orange – generosity
Orange-blossom – chastity

Pansy – thoughts
Parsley – festivity
Pasque flower – you have no claims
Penny royal – flee away
Peony – anger
Petunia – never despair
Peppermint – cordiality
Pimpernel – change
Pink – boldness
Poplar – courage
Poppy, field – consolation
Primrose, red – unpatronized merit
Primula – animation

Quaking grass – agitation

Rhododendron – danger
Rose, damask – freshness
Rose, moss – superior merit
Rose, musk – a capricious beauty
Rose, rambler – only deserve my love
Rose, red bud – you are young and beautiful
Rose, white – I am worthy of you
Rose, white bud – a heart ignorant of love
Rose, yellow – departure of love

Saffron – marriage
Sage – domestic virtue
Salvia, blue – I think of you
Salvia, red – forever thine
Scabious – unfortunate love
Snowdrop – hope
Southernwood – merriment
Stock – promptitude
Sunflower – haughtiness
Sweet cicely – gladness
Sweet pea – departure
Sycamore – curiosity

Tamarisk – crime
Tansy, wild – I do declare war against you
Teasel – Misanthropy
Thistle – austerity
Tulip, red – declaration of love

Valerian – accommodating disposition
Verbena – enchantment
Vine – intoxication
Violet, blue – faithfulness
Violet, white – modesty

Wall flower – fidelity
Wheat – prosperity
Willow, weeping – mourning
Wisteria – regret
Witch hazel – a spell
Wood sorrel – joy
Wormwood – absence

Xeranthemum – cheerfulness under adversity

Zinnia – thoughts of absent friends

USEFUL ADDRESSES

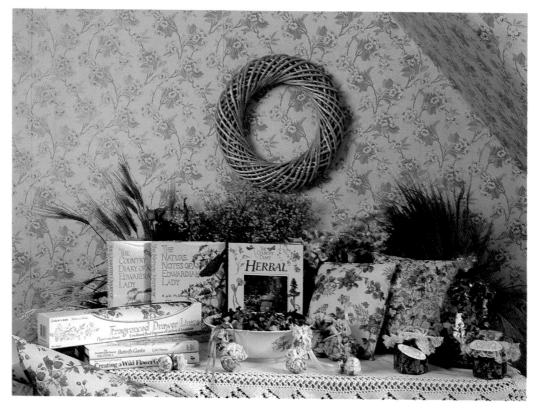

The fragranced drawer liners, herb pillows and pot pourri, as shown here, are available from Kitty Little Ltd of Stoke-on-Trent. Other *Country Diary* merchandise is available through most good department stores.

Please send a stamped addressed envelope when contacting any of the following UK manufacturers. For US addresses see separate lists.

DRIED FLOWER SHOPS

HAY FEVER
4 Cathedral Close
Exeter
Devon EX1 1EZ
Tel: 0392 56578

Retail only; supplies dried flowers, florist's accessories, basketware, pot pourri and oils

HARRODS
Knightsbridge
London SW1X 7XL
Tel: 071 730 1234

Dried flower bunches

HILLIER & HILTON
98 Church Road
Barnes
London SW13 0DG
Tel: 081 748 1810

Specialist dried flower shop

DAISY CHAIN
58 Street Lane
Roundhay
Leeds OS8 2DQ
Tel: 0532 663039

Specialist dried flower shop

THE FLOWER BASKET
25 Frankwell
Shrewsbury
Shropshire SY3 8JY
Tel: 0743 58034

Specialist dried flower shop

ARABELLA
Green Park Station
Bath
Avon BA1 1JB
Tel: 0225 331888

Specialist dried flower shop

DRIED FLOWER SUPPLIERS

MR & MRS V. TAYLOR
The Round House
Park Hatch
Lox Hill
Godalming
Surrey GU8 4BL
Tel: 048649 375

Specialists in beautiful home-grown flowers; wholesale and retail

CUT AND DRIED
Balls Farm Growers
Balls Farm Road

Ide
Devon EX2 9RA
Tel: 0392 75696

Home-grown flowers as well as imported dried flowers

SAVANNAH MARKETING
60 Bishops Road
Clevedon
Bristol BS19 4NG
Tel: 0934 835149

Specialists in African flowers and English roses preserved in silica gel

HOLLAND AND EVANS LTD
Chesterton House
Chesterton
Near Bridgnorth
Shropshire WV15 5NX
Tel: 07465 445/6/7

Wholesalers of dried flowers, basketware and ribbons

R. & R. FLOWERS
Portland House
51 Colney Hatch Lane
Muswell Hill
London N10 1LJ
Tel: 081 883 9123

Specialists in African flowers

WHOLESALE BASKETWARE

A & S DESIGNS
26 Acton Park Industrial Estate
Stanley Gardens
The Vale
London W3 7QE
Tel: 081 743 6060

Good quality baskets and garlands
from around the world

SUPPLIERS OF POT POURRI

MEADOW HERBS LTD
Premier Place
Abbey Park
Romsey
Hampshire SO51 9AQ
Tel: 0794 830766

Suppliers of ready-made pot
pourri, pot pourri kits and essential
oils; retail and wholesale

ESSENTIAL OILS

NEALS YARD REMEDIES
Neal's Yard
Covent Garden
London WC2
Tel: 071 284 2039

Essential oils to both the trade
and retail

CULPEPPER LTD
21 Bruton Street
London W1X 7DA
Tel: 071 629 4559

Essential oils, spices and herbs

PLANT SUPPLIERS

PETER BEALES ROSES
London Road
Attleborough
Norfolk NR17 1AY
Tel: 0953 454707

Old and species roses

KELWAYS NURSERIES LTD
Langport
Somerset TA10 9SL
Tel: 0458 250521

Specialists in peonies

THE COTTAGE GARDEN
SOCIETY
Old Hall Cottage
Pump Lane
Churton
Chester CH3 6LR

Cottage garden seed and
plant exchange

LANDLIFE WILD FLOWER LTD
The Old Police Station
Lark Lane
Liverpool L17 8UU
Tel: 051 728 7011

Wildflower plants and seeds

OAK COTTAGE HERB GARDEN
Nesscliff
Shrewsbury
Shropshire SY4 1DB
Tel: 0743 81262

Specialists in herb plants

THE ROCK HOUSE HERB FARM
Dunsford
Devon EX6 7EP
Tel: 0647 52514

Wholesale and retail fresh-cut herbs

SUFFOLK HERBS LTD
Sawyer's Farm
Little Cornard
Sudbury
Suffolk CO10 0NY
Tel: 0787 227247

Wildflower plants and seeds

NPK LANDSCAPE ARCHITECTS
542 Parrs Wood Road
East Didsbury
Manchester M20 0QA
Tel: 061 794 9314

Native wildflower and bulb
specialists

WILDFLOWER SEED SPECIALISTS

JOHN CHAMBERS
15 Westleigh Road
Barton Seagrave
Kettering
Northamptonshire NN15 5AJ
Tel: 0933 681632

Packeted seed and conservation
mixtures

THE SEED BANK
Cowcombe Farm
Gipsy Lane
Chalford
Stroud
Gloucestershire GL6 8HP

Packeted seed and seed exchange

PRESSED FLOWERS

JOANNA SHEEN LTD
7 Lucius Street
Torquay
Devon TQ2 5UW
Tel: 0803 201311

Retails individual pressed flowers,
pressed-flower pictures and dried
flower bunches; special courses on
pressing flowers

DRYAD
P.O. Box 38
Northgates
Leicester LE1 9BU

Flower presses; write for stockists

ART PAPERS

FAULKNER FINE ART PAPERS
76 Southampton Row
London WC1

Hand made paper; inks and pens

PAPERCHASE
Tottenham Court Road
London

Art supplies, specialist papers and
cards

PICTURE FRAMING

TALISMAN FRAMING
Salterton Workshop
Station Road
Budleigh Salterton
Devon EX9 6RJ
Tel: 03954 2251

Comprehensive picture-framing
service

USEFUL ADDRESSES FOR READERS IN THE UNITED STATES

SOURCES FOR HERBS AND DRIED FLOWERS

PECONIC RIVER HERB FARM
310-C River Road
Calverton
New York 11933
(516) 369-0058

Nearly 400 kinds of herbs and dried
flowers; specialize in everlastings;
Saturday classes March-November;
no mail order

SANDY MUSH HERB NURSERY
Route 2, Surrett Cove Road
Leicester
North Carolina 28748
(704) 683-2014

Nearly 900 items; seeds and plants
available by mail; send $4 for
catalogue

TAYLOR'S HERB GARDENS, INC.
1535 Lone Oak Road
Vista
California 92084
(619) 727-3485

Plants and seeds available by mail;
guaranteed live arrival of healthy
plants everywhere in the U.S.;
catalogue free

THE HERB COTTAGE
Washington Cathedral
Massachusetts & Wisconsin Aves. NW
Washington, D.C. 20016-5098
(202) 537-8982

Dried herbs and seeds available by
mail; catalogue free

VAL'S NATURALS
P.O. Box 832
Kathleen, Florida 33849
(813) 858-8991

Specializes in imported dried rose buds and red pepper berries for pot pourri; minimum order required

WELL-SWEEP HERB FARM
317 Mt. Bethel Road
Port Murray
New Jersey 07865
(201) 852-5390

Herbs, seeds, dried flowers, and pot pourri supplies available by mail; send $2 for catalogue

SOURCES FOR ROSES

ROSES OF YESTERDAY AND TODAY
802 Brown's Valley Road
Watsonville
California 95076
(408) 724-3537

Rose bushes available by mail; send $3 for catalogue (3rd class mail) or $4 for catalogue (1st class mail)

WAYSIDE GARDENS
Hodges
South Carolina 29695-0001
(803) 223-1968

A wide variety of quality plants and roses; highly respected; catalogue free; all items available by mail

ESSENTIAL OILS

CASWELL-MASSEY CO.
Catalogue Division
Dover
Delaware
(800) 326-0500

About 20 different flavors including fern, gardenia, honeysuckle, rose jasmine, and lavender

STORES:
518 Lexington Avenue
New York City
New York
(212) 755-2254

South Street Seaport
New York City
New York
(212) 608-5401

World Financial Center
New York City
New York
(212) 945-2630

Albany
New York
(518) 452-1443

Atlanta
Georgia
(404) 261-9415

Boca Raton
Florida
(407) 338-0999

Miami
Florida
(305) 255-3899

Winter Park
Florida
(407) 647-2455

San Diego
California
(619) 233-6015

Santa Ana
California
(714) 972-0380

San Francisco
California
(415) 681-6006

Newport Beach
California
(714) 640-6750

CHERCHEZ
862 Lexington Avenue
New York City
New York
(212) 737-8215

A wide selection including bergamot, geranium, honeysuckle, lemon verbena, lily of the valley, old English rose, field flowers, and 16th century rondelitia

HOVÉ PARFUMEUR, LTD
824 Royal Street
New Orleans
Louisiana
(504) 525-7827

Rose jasmine and lavender

ACKNOWLEDGEMENTS

This book has been enormous fun to research and write, and I wish to thank everyone who has been so extremely kind and who has helped so generously. First, I want to thank Simon McBride. This is the second book we have worked on together, and I think his photography is absolutely stunning: he takes such immense care with each photo that he always captures just the right atmosphere in his pictures. I also wish to thank Lydia Darbyshire for editing the book so beautifully and understanding the subject with such ease. I want to thank Sue Stainton for her wonderfully creative designing and for transforming all our hard work into a book! My thanks, too, to Mathew Eyett Wright of Art History Design, not only for his delightful illustrations but to him and his wife, Julie, for lending us their house for so many of the photographs that appear in the book.

I also want to thank Diana and Hugo Breitmeyer for their great kindness and hospitality in lending us their house and gardens. I would also like to thank the following friends and family for their help: Fiona Orde: Diana Baxter: Jo and Annie Baker: Dr and Mrs Elzik: my brother John and his wife Sue for the many photos taken in their cottage: my mother: Jessica for her ancient bicycle; and Marie Mathews, who was so kind, enthusiastic and hospitable in lending us her beautiful home. Also grateful thanks to Susie Cove, whose seaside home has to be in one of the most enviable locations in Devon and where we began our photos, and, finally, to Mr and Mrs Taylor, who let us photograph their exquisite garden which is really the most lovely walled garden I have ever seen – the flowers were overwhelming and so was their kindness.

Several suppliers were also kind enough to provide ingredients for my book. Thank you to Joanna Sheen for helping me with her exquisite pressed flowers; Jim Rushbrook of Meadow Herbs for supplying wonderful pot pourri ingredients; and Richard Hutt for his help in supplying fresh herbs.

INDEX

Page numbers in *italics* refer to captions to photographs and line illustrations. Only main references to, and illustrations of, individual flowers and plants are indexed.

A cottage door decorated with a mixed bouquet made with tilancia (moss), winter viburnum and pittosporum preserved with glycerine, cornflowers, hydrangeas, helipterum (acroclinium) daisies, peonies, roses, amaranthus, achillea, marjoram, blue larkspur, mimosa and helichrysum and tied together with thick garden string to add to the rustic effect.